Contents

FOR PENELOPE HEIN UNRUH

Acknowledgments

This study is based on the sociological ideas and practical experiences of many people. Therefore, I owe both intellectual and personal debts. I would first like to thank the many older people in Northern California who freely shared their time and experiences. While they often did not understand how their lives might be sociologically interesting and important, they humored me and were most gracious in sharing their thoughts and feelings.

Through the research and writing, John Lofland was always encouraging. He freely shared ideas and insights with regard to social worlds, the aged, and the analytic process. Lyn Lofland first impressed me with the importance of studying urban social organization. She continued offering valuable insight and editorial advice. Anselm Strauss, whose continued interest in the value of analyzing social worlds has been an inspiration, freely shared ideas through personal conversation and various unpublished manuscripts. Carroll Estes offered insightful advice and support concerning the place of this research in the fields of sociology and gerontology. Her substantive suggestions and editorial advice are valued. As editor of the "Sociological Observations" series, John Johnson offered much needed advice and support. I would also like to thank John Walton, Peter Hall, Victor Marshall, Vern Bengtson, Leonard Cain, and Marshall Graney, who commented on various portions of this study. Their contributions are noticeable and valuable. Bernadette Tarallo, Thomas Dietz, and Juanita Wood never failed in their ability to offer support, advice, and pleasant diversions. I would also like to extend an overdue note of thanks to my parents for their support and encouragement over the years. As always, Penelope Hein Unruh was remarkably patient, interested, and encouraging.

Finally, the early stages of project formulation and fieldwork were facilitated by a Regents Fellowship in the Department of Sociology at the University of California, Davis. Final revisions of the study for publication were completed during the beginning of my appointment as a Postdoctoral Fellow in a National Institute of Mental Health Advanced Training Program in Mental Health Evaluation Research (USPHS MH-14583) in the Department of Sociology at the University of California, Los Angeles.

Foreword

Invisible Lives makes important contributions, I believe, both to social gerontology and to the sociology of organizational life. It makes these contributions through an empirically grounded and close scrutiny of older citizens' activities as they participate in various kinds of social worlds including leisure, collector, performance, and occupational worlds. In making this examination David Unruh presents us with a new perspective on the study and understanding of the lives of older people. The prevailing conceptions of aging emphasize the gradual falling away of the aging from participation in meaningful institutions and organizations; they are not as well integrated into society as younger people. The notion of integration is carefully examined here, and prevailing conceptions based on it are cogently criticized for their overlooking of how older people may actually live satisfying and even exciting lives through various types of involvements that have either escaped the notice of gerontologists or not been properly assessed for their significance. The key to integration for many people, not merely for the aged but including them — for surely they are like most of us, most of the time — is that they may engage in activities not necessarily falling under the conventional rubrics of family, occupation, or organization — which assuredly often play a smaller part in their lives than when they were younger.

Through a number of vivid case histories, as well as through analytic discussions, David Unruh shows how the elderly achieve or maintain integration through their behavioral and symbolic participation in a variety of social worlds. He quite properly emphasizes how they may move in and through and out of those worlds, depending on many circumstances: so that we gain a picture of nonstatic involvement — where the search for new involvements is as rewarding frequently as "simply finding stability through social integration" of the more visible kind.

Readers will discover many specific findings in these pages that will interest them. Among the ones that struck me were these: Integration into social worlds based primarily on personal relations with other participants rather than on the activities performed "is a risky proposition," especially as people move along in the life cycle; and among the conditions for seeking out new worlds is being hit by a chronic illness, for then symptoms make certain activities difficult or impossible, yet a host of others may be learned and enjoyed; and senior citizen centers may introduce their members into various new activities without encouragement to actually move into contact with social worlds where those activities are central, thus, the seniors miss opportunities to make contact with people of all ages who seriously share in those activities and within a much wider sphere of communal action.

In using the concept of social world to study the lives of older Americans, David Unruh has also illuminated unexplored or insufficiently understood aspects of social worlds. Thus, he offers a useful classification of this phenomenon. And quite properly in emphasizing the activity core of these worlds, he has shown how members become linked with them by virtue of their degrees of participation. A useful classification of types of participation is also given us. Attention is directed to the various mixes of generation that exist within different social worlds. In general, Unruh's analysis counteracts the prevailing social science focus on perhaps over-studied institutional and formal organizational life; this is done by pointing to the more fluid membership and more permeable, if not necessarily more evanescent, social groupings. With the evolution of increasing international travel, international media, and a multitude of associations that cross national boundaries, it is perfectly predictable that social worlds and their memberships will receive more and more — and well deserved — research attention from social scientists. This book is a small step in that direction but a suggestive one.

— Anselm Strauss
University of California, San Francisco

INTRODUCTION

THE NOTION OF SOCIAL WORLDS

The notion of a *social world* has intrigued me ever since I first read the work of Robert E. Park and his many students. At the University of Chicago, during the early years of American sociology, Park used the term to describe shared cultural elements and organized outlooks that tend to arise among people sharing common orientations and experiences in social life. For example, Paul Cressey (1932) described the taxi-dance hall as a distinct social world that maintained a special internal logic, a set of unique activities, an idiosyncratic vocabulary, and other cultural elements in modern urban society. While the early Chicago sociologists offered rich descriptions of city life, it is unfortunate that conceptual precision and theory-building often were lacking. The research tradition of the Chicago school, rich in empirical description, has been passed on to many contemporary ethnographers, urban sociologists, and others interested in contemporary city life. Similarly, a fair amount of contemporary research rooted in this naturalistic research tradition also may be characterized by its conceptual imprecision and theoretical blindness.

Since the term social world has been employed as a descriptive device rather than developed as a sociological concept, it has acquired a variety of imprecise and common-sense meanings. For example, we are likely to hear or read about the "worlds" of ballet, theater, politics, and sport on the evening news or in popular magazines. Perhaps because the term is so deeply ingrained in the lexicon of everyday life, few people are likely to ponder the meaning, imagery, and definition of a social world. Similarly, sociologists have referred to worlds of the poor, the working classes, the married, the divorced, and the elderly without understanding (or acknowledging) the presumably shared cultural elements that unite these people into common worlds. More often than not, these studies are cohort analyses based on demographic variables, which are assumed to imply shared perspectives and a common culture among people. Therefore, the shared perspectives and orientations so vital to the Chicago sociologists' use of the term are taken for granted without empirical evidence, or overlain onto the experiences of disparate individuals (see Damon, 1977; Hunt, 1966; Rose, 1965; Smith, 1966).

Further complicating matters, phenomenologists have used the term to refer to various orders of reality, subuniverses of human experience, or finite provinces of meaning in which humans carve out their existence in the modern world (see Berger and Luckmann, 1966; Husserl, 1950; Schutz, 1962). Edmund Husserl (1950), for example, spoke of "our everyday life-world" as the world that people experience at every point of their existence as "immediately and simply given." It is a world taken for granted and of practical interest to human beings. In an effort that implies a potential merger between the Chicago School and phenomenological understandings of the term, Benita Luckmann observed that

> In late industrial society the segment of the life-world actually "inhabited" by man consists of many small worlds. These are located within the "private" as well as the institutional spheres of existence. Though of different degrees of importance and necessity of man's existence, none of them represents a "whole" life-world in which all of man's life unfolds. One can rather speak of man's part-time existence in part-time societies. To describe tentatively the multi-dimensional nature of everyday life in contemporary society I shall speak of the small life-worlds of man [1970: 581].

In essence, people in modern urban society are not integrated into a single social world wherein all personal meaning is located, but rather in many social worlds that encourage segmentation of the life-round.

Therefore, personal meaning in urban society is likely derived out of a combination of many social involvements, roles, and relationships (see Kornhauser, 1959; Riesman et al., 1950).

It is precisely the segmented nature of modern social life that encouraged the sociologists Tamotsu Shibutani and Anselm Strauss to revive the Chicago school notion of social worlds and overlay symbolic interactionist imagery. Specifically, during the 1950s Shibutani emphasized matters of process and personal meaning based on lines of shared communication among actors. Modern urban societies, then, are made up of a bewildering array of social worlds which arise out of shared communication. Social worlds are "universes of regularized response" built up by people in interaction with one another (Shibutani, 1955: 565). In contrast with the conventional phenomenological use of the term, social worlds live on and function outside the minds of individuals. They may not continue on exactly the same course as they once did, but they do have a concrete, objective quality about them. For example, the art world lives on even after the deaths of Picasso, Monet, and Peggy Guggenheim. The value of their work or contributions may have changed or been redefined, but the art world continues nonetheless.

Simultaneously frustrated with the absence of empirical research focused on social worlds and excited about the usefulness of the concept, Anselm Strauss (see 1961, 1962, 1967) repeatedly issued a call for sociologists to study seriously the emergence of social worlds. In the 1970s and 1980s Strauss began formulating a social world perspective heavily steeped in George Herbert Mead's view of society. Mead emphasized the endless formation of universes of discourse that produced "a metaphor of groups emerging, evolving, developing, splintering, disintegrating, or coalescing with others to form new groups" (Strauss, 1978a: 121, see also Mead, 1934).

The concept of social worlds has become increasingly refined over the past decade. We now understand that social worlds coalesce around the production, creation, distribution, and evaluation of various "social objects" (see McCall and Simmons, 1978: 50). Through the coordinated efforts of people, the social objects of art, stamps, bicycles, classical music, surfing, and so on are created and demand the time and energy of many. This burgeoning analytic perspective has been useful in understanding the social organization of such diverse activities as computing (Kling and Gerson, 1978), alcoholism (Weiner, 1981), chronic pain (Fagerhaugh and Strauss, 1977), belly dancing (Suczek, 1977), liquor production (Denzin, 1977; 1978), and photography (Rosenblum, 1978.)[1] The most complete and sophisticated substantive analysis of the definition, creation, production, and distribution of a social object is Howard Becker's (1982) study of art worlds.

I believe that greater conceptual precision and theoretical development of the concept *social world* can only be brought about by analyzing the phenomenon as a distinct form of social organization. Defined as it will be employed throughout this study: *A social world is an extremely large, highly permeable, amorphous, and spatially transcendant form of social organization wherein actors are linked cognitively through shared perspectives arising out of common channels of communication.* For example, the art world is a system of ideas, practices, events, and procedures that meaningfully link people across the boundaries of neighborhoods, cities, regions, states, and nations. The boundaries are neither easily seen nor defined. Rather, it is the access to information about activities and processes in this social world that facilitates or limits personal integration.

In this study, my concern is to explore and analyze the integration of individuals into various social worlds. Such integration has largely been overlooked in the sociological literature.[2] The reasons for the omission may be many, but I believe it is because the primary basis for personal integration differs from those that bind people into conventional forms of social organization. For example, an examination of the scope and content of social integration studies reveals a heavy emphasis on *families, informal groups, interest groups, complex organizations, territorial communities,* and *voluntary associations.* These are the forms that have caught our sociological eye and dominated empirical research.[3] These forms tend to unite and coalesce around what I have termed "conventional bases," which serve as the predominant links among actors. Thus, while all forms of social organization demand a certain degree of cognitive identification, matters of *spatial contiguity, formal membership, rational-bureaucratic lines,* and *innate or ascribed traits* loom large in the social integration of people into those conventional forms. In contrast, a social world entirely depends upon the influence of communication and the cognitive state of those who would be involved. Since the tentacles of modern communication have extended to all corners of modern society, the social world has become a pervasive and eminently important form of social organization (see Fischer, 1976, 1982; Irwin, 1970a; Lofland, 1975; Strauss, 1978a).

PROBLEMATIC POPULATIONS

How can the study of this pervasive and eminently important form of social organization help us understand the social integration of people in modern society? In an important way, the focus on personal integration in social worlds illuminates and helps us better understand a portion of people's lives generally overlooked in most social science accounts. It is an endeavor that looks more at where actors focus their attention, derive their identities, and locate a portion of their total resources than those that emphasize the physical locations, formal memberships, bureaucratic roles, and kinship ties of the people studied. While these factors are important, they represent only a portion of that which meaningfully links modern actors.

The notion of *invisible lives* now comes into play. Since social worlds and the role of communication in binding social actors together has not received widespread recognition, the lives of people in this form of social organization are indeed invisible. Integration into social worlds is invisible also because the activities, processes, and actions that link people together often are not performed publicly. People who read newsletters, watch television, listen to the radio, devise videotapes, write letters, use telephones, and the like tend to do so alone or in the company of others with similar interests. These activities often are privately accomplished outside the cognizance of others. Similarly, the questions sociologists tend to ask about social integration generally are not attuned to phenomena such as social worlds where formal membership is not crucial, formal roles include only a small proportion of participants, and territorial boundaries are easily transcended.

The study of invisible lives in social worlds is best directed toward what I have termed *problematic populations*. That is, there are certain populations, cohorts, or groups of people who (for various reasons) are believed to find integration and involvement in society

especially problematic. A quick overview of the sociological literature would reveal the mentally ill, the physically disabled, minority
group members, the institutionalized, and the deinstitutionalized to
be examples of such populations.

Perhaps most important among these problematic populations are
the aged in modern society. Unlike the traits or factors that selectively
render other populations problematic, all of us must face the prospect
of growing old. Coupled with the fact that the 11% of the U. S.
population 65 years of age and over is increasing in sheer numbers and
proportions, sociological awareness of the aged has been heightened.
The aged may, in fact, be *the* symbol of the 1980s (see Estes, 1979;
Tindale and Marshall, 1980).

Throughout this study, I will be concerned with a number of issues
common to sociological analyses of the aged. For example, the status
and treatment of older people within a variety of social worlds is a
major concern. Similarly, the effects of advancing age will be explored
with regard to changes in personal integration, as well as the
emergence or decline of specific social worlds. Finally, old age in
modern society is accompanied by losses of various kinds: the death
of a spouse, forced retirement, scarce economic resources, declining
physical abilities, and perhaps the onset of chronic illness. The effects
of these and other losses on integration into social worlds will be a
theme interwoven throughout the analysis.

At times, it may appear as though the older people portrayed in
this study differ little from those of any age who have suffered social
losses. This is exactly a major conclusion of this study. The expectation that the aged are qualitatively different is so pervasive in everyday life that statements that claim the contrary stand out and
become noteworthy (see Keith, 1982: 2). Older people seem to experience and understand the world much like all people in similar
social, cultural, and historical conditions.

With this in mind, I believe the substantive focus and theoretical
framework of *Invisible Lives* should be useful to a broad range of
audiences. It is most apparent that knowledge about social worlds of
the aged would be useful to sociologists of aging, social gerontologists, and their students. I have attempted to present a readable
portrait of older people and a major aspect of their lives in modern
urban society. Less obvious, but no less important, this study should

also have relevance for those interested in urban social organization, social interaction, and symbolic interaction. Through the extensive use of "theoretical footnotes," I will expand upon and clarify some of the more abstract qualities of social worlds and those who are integrated within them.

OVERVIEW OF THE STUDY

The first order of business in analyzing social worlds of the aged is to focus on the broader issue of social integration in old age. The notion of social integration often is taken for granted among gerontologists, with the assumption being that it is rather easily determined, understood, and evaluated. Throughout Chapter 1 the notion of social integration is rendered problematic. A number of analytic strategies are introduced with regard to this matter, and then the focus shifts to the integration of older people in social worlds. The study of integration into social worlds requires a perspective and an approach attuned to the nature of the social organizational form. This discussion concludes with an overview of the research process, fieldwork techniques, and the process of analyzing interview materials.

Social world involvements often provide the aged with memories by which the past is preserved and with activities to organize the present. By analyzing social worlds in aging lives, Chapter 2 is first concerned with the effects of increased awareness of death on the personal meaning older people derive from various social worlds. A corollary concern is the way social world integration changes as the life cycle progresses and old age approaches. If particular social worlds are to remain meaningful across the life cycle, the aged must struggle to keep the intense interest, physical stamina, and mental abilities often required in the face of their age peers dropping by the wayside through disability, illness, lack of interest, or death.

In Chapter 3 the analysis shifts to the aged in specific social worlds. While social worlds tend to include actors of many ages, some are best characterized by the predominance of one age group over others. Social worlds may be characterized as youthful, age-mixed, and older depending upon the proportion and centrality of various age groups. Integration of the aged, and the evaluation of their involvement, is quite different in each of these worlds. To some degree, however, matters of chronological age are downplayed or concealed in social worlds since integration and involvement may be maintained through media of various kinds.

The evaluation of the aged in social worlds continues in Chapter 4, and a set of eight "integrating activities" is introduced that codifies the ways by which older people maintain integration. The activities available to the aged depend upon the character of specific worlds, proportion of elderly involved, and various age-related factors. The nature of the experience and the kinds of knowledge acquired by the aged greatly depend upon the activities by which they are integrated.

In Chapter 5 I introduce a set of four social types *(strangers, tourists, regulars,* and *insiders)* that captures the experiences of the aged as they become integrated into this form of social organization. The kind of knowledge the aged have regarding the activities of a social world and the degree to which they are integrated are reflected in the matters of committment, perception, and personal meaning.

Integration as social process, implied throughout earlier chapters, is the subject of Chapter 6. The routes by which the major figures in this study changed and modified their integration in various social worlds are analyzed by using the earlier described set of four social types. Social integration does not imply static involvement. Instead, the aged clearly are portrayed as moving in, through, and out of many social worlds. For some older people the search for new involvements is as rewarding as finding stability in social integration.

In the final chapter the invisible lives of the aged become the object of further reflection and consideration. I will discuss the implications of the study for understanding the lives of the aged in modern society, broadening the concept of social integration in social gerontology, and understanding the importance of social world involvement. Finally, I will review the prospects and possibilities for future research.

NOTES

1. It should be noted that the emerging social world perspective developed by Anselm Strauss is an explicit attempt to address the popular critique that symbolic interactionists fail to study macro-social organization (see Maines, 1977). It is a

perspective that evolved out of the study of "negotiated order" in and among complex organizations (see Bucher and Strauss, 1961; Strauss et al., 1964; Strauss, 1978a).

2. In recent decades a number of theoretical schemes and empirical works have appeared that focus on social organization, which is characterized as extremely large, highly permeable, amorphous, and spatially transcendent. I specifically refer to those studies focusing on social networks (Granovetter, 1974; Laumann and Pappi, 1976; Mitchell, 1969), subcultures (Arnold, 1970; Cohen, 1955; Fine and Kleinman, 1979; Fischer, 1982; Gordon, 1947; Irwin, 1970a), invisible colleges (Crane, 1972; Mullins, 1968; 1973; Price, 1963), communities within communities (Goode, 1957), ecologies of games (Long, 1958), activity systems (Irwin, 1977), behavior systems (Hollingshead, 1939) social circles (Kadushin, 1966; 1968; 1976), and certain treatments of social movements (Gerlach and Hine, 1970). The subcultural tradition is the most widely developed among the schemes listed. It is a tradition that dates back to the work of Frederic Thrasher (1927), Edwin Sutherland (1939), and August Hollingshead (1939) and has achieved current popularity in studies of a broad range of phenomena. The concept recently was reconceptualized so as to bring it more into line with my use of the concept social world. Gary Alan Fine and Sheryl Kleinman (1979) have emphasized the shared communication and self identification among those who would be involved. Unlike many other researchers, they have not assumed that subcultures are homogeneous, closed social entities isolated from the larger society. Instead, change is viewed as endemic and facilitated by interlocking group culture, structural roles, and media diffusion. In contrast, the social network approach has achieved widespread popularity and is characterized by sophisticated modeling and other quantitative procedures. It is interesting to note that many network theorists construct their elaborate schemes by asking people to identify important contacts and to rate their importance (Granovetter, 1975; Mullins, 1968; 1973; Price, 1963; 1965; White et al., 1976). However, an overly heavy reliance on the verbal reports of actors may present problems in constructing accurate social networks. H. R. Bernard and P. D. Killworth (1976, 1977) have amassed much evidence which calls the accuracy of such information into question. It seems that when compared with an objective measure like monitoring telephone calls, most people are not very accurate in remembering nor rank ordering their social contacts.

3. While these forms of social organization dominate sociological thought, they are not exhaustive of the possibilities for discovering other forms of social organization. Sociologist Lyn Lofland maintains that dominance of the territorial definition of community has had two consequences: "(1) It has led to an overemphasis on a restricted range of empirical settings — those to which the model might reasonably apply and (2) It has led to the restriction of vision relative to the possible empirical varieties of urban social organization, to a failure of creative imagination relative to the possible relationships that humans can have to one another in and through and across space" (1975: 151-152).

1

SOCIAL INTEGRATION IN
OLD AGE

The study of social integration in old age has been a major focus of much sociological and gerontological research over the past three decades. These studies make up a significant body of research, and represent the niche in social gerontology within which the social worlds of the aged should be placed. However, despite the large number of studies focused on matters of social integration, few people have stopped to consider the definition and meaning of the term. For example, what does social integration mean? How do social gerontologists know it when they see it in the lives of the aged? What is the empirical evidence of its presence or absence? How is social integration achieved and accomplished by older individuals? Finally, what kinds and degrees of social integration exist? In effect, use of the term often is imprecise, unclear, and occasionally restrictive. Therefore, a brief discussion of social integration must serve as the point of departure. An overview of current approaches and generalizations regarding social integration in old age provides the necessary background for developing this look at the "invisible lives" of older people in social worlds. Thus, by adopting a reflexive posture toward the matter of social integration, a better understanding of the subject and approach of this research will be developed.

THE NOTION OF SOCIAL INTEGRATION

The term "social integration" is widely used by social gerontologists and sociologists of aging to describe both the focus of empirical research and its presumed relevance or application to everyday situations. In scholarly practice, then, the term refers to the actual empirical study of the integration of older people into society in its many forms, and the ameliorative strategies designed to enhance or facilitate social integration. Thus, a certain amount of ambiguity exists regarding the meaning and intent implied by the term.

Irving Rosow (1967; 1974) has developed the most comprehensive definition and study of social integration in old age. In his view, "the integration of individuals into their society results from forces which place them within the system and govern their participation and patterned associations with others" (1967: 9). Social values, group memberships, and social roles are conceived as the axes providing the ties that structure social interaction, place the person in society, and order relations with others. In effect, actors are integrated into society through the beliefs they hold, the positions they occupy, and the groups to which they belong. While the work of most social gerontologists basically conforms to Rosow's conception, few have been as explicit in their study of social integration.[1]

For the aged, the general belief has been that satisfactory social integration might be maintained to the extent that middle age patterns are preserved in the face of advancing age. The assumption being that people are well integrated during their middle years and become less so over the years. In other words, old age carries with it the potential for drastic changes with regard to the maintenance of social roles and group memberships (Blau, 1961, 1973; Lockwood, 1964; Townsend, 1957). For example, aging often brings with it losses of central social roles resulting from status changes in the arenas of marriage, work, family, income, health, and the like. Group memberships also tend to decline with age. Social gerontologists have long chronicled the decreasing participation and commitment of older people in formal organizations, voluntary associations, and other community involvements (see Rosow, 1974; Litwak and Szelenyi, 1969; Smith, 1966). The social values of older people, on the other hand, tend to be more stable across the life span and less susceptible to change through social loss and societal pressure (see Bengtson and Kuypers, 1971;

Neugarten, 1970). The bulk of research on social integration, then, has focused on changes in social roles and group memberships, and has downplayed the matter of social values.

In a sense, the many studies of isolation among the aged represent a look at the dark side of social integration. That is, the emphasis in this research is not on the degree to which older people have maintained ties and linkages with others, but on the extent to which they have not (see Bennett, 1980, 1973; Lowenthal, 1964; Lowenthal and Robinson, 1976). Focused mostly on the ill and institutionalized aged, research on social isolation pays special heed and gives special importance to face-to-face contact. That is, the aged are perceived to be isolated if they have not had sufficient number of contacts in a specified period of time. Isolation is perceived as accurately describing aging lives when "they have not been chosen by anyone as an associate in community activities or relations" (Lundberg and Lawsing, 1949), interpersonal relationships appear attenuated (Clausen and Kohn, 1954; Turnstall, 1966), or when they appear to have a small number of weekly social contacts (Bennett, 1980; Blau, 1973; Rodstein et al., 1976; Townsend, 1957).

It is necessary to look more closely at some factors mentioned in the literature said to pull the aged out of satisfactory social integration and pull them into social isolation. For example, one of the things unique to aging is "the fact that the entire age cohort becomes increasingly frail" (Dono et al., 1979). While great individual variation exists, many older people find it increasingly difficult to maintain friendships, neighborhood ties, family relationships, and the like under these conditions. The deaths of friends or spouses and further restrictions on mobility continually reduce opportunities for social integration (see Lopata, 1973, 1979). Even when the aged manage to overcome demographic, social, and physical obstacles and establish new relationships, the quality of the new marriages, friendships, neighborhood ties, and the like may not equal those of the past. The aged are not likely to have extensive shared pasts, engage in long-term planning, nor develop comparable levels of commitment toward others in these new groups (Dono et al., 1979: 412).[2] Institutionalization is another factor that may push the aged toward social isolation. In nursing homes, long-term care hospitals, homes for the aged, and the like, contacts and associations with others may be limited and fewer in number.

Retirement and the accompanying reduction of income also affects the nature and degree of social integration (Schulz, 1980; Streib, 1974). In general, the aged find themselves with fewer resources to exchange than working people (see Dowd, 1975; Sussman, 1965). Consequently, the aged are unable to extend the kinds of aid they might have in the past. This reduces their social value and may result in diminished social contacts and involvement with others. Further, reduced income places limitations on mobility, contact with others, and the kinds of leisure activities that might be pursued.

Finally, there are a number of other factors influencing social integration in old age. Arnold Rose (1965) argued that social pressures and life conditions experienced by the aged may result in unique life styles, social roles, and interpersonal stresses. Consequently, the importance of age peers in supplying sources of support and knowledge in social life was believed to magnify in old age. The negative societal view of the aged, which Robert Butler (1969) has termed "ageism," may further push older people away from age-heterogeneous involvements and pull them toward age segregation. This phenomenon is reflected in the many neighborhoods, housing units, and retirement communities populated by older people.

In approaching the study of social integration, most social researchers have adopted a restricted range of methods and approaches. The empirical questions they ask, for example, have focused on the presence or absence of involvements in a restricted range of social involvements. Informal groups, families, territorial communities, voluntary associations, and formal organizations head the list of social forms taken into consideration when evaluating social integration; the point being that the range of involvements used to indicate acceptable social integration is unnecessarily narrow. For example, the phenomenon of social world involvement lying at the heart of this study would not arise out of questions focused on other forms. Therefore, the elaborate tables and statistical manipulations favored by many social gerontologists capture only selected aspects of social integration in old age.

Additional deficiencies arise with regard to indicators of integration or isolation. Many factors have been explored that influence social integration in old age. Yet conventional survey and questionnaire approaches tend to freeze social action and capture involvement at a single point in time. Thus, integration tends to become an "either/or" proposition with little attention given to the fact that older people often move in and out of many involvements, change modes of participation to match various constraints, and journey among a broad range of activities that contribute to social integration.

In essence, at least three conceptual problems seem to characterize the literature on social integration in old age: (1) In definition and usage, the term social integration is undefined or vaguely identified as a network of bonds that include shared values, group memberships, and social roles; (2) Conceptions of facilitants and constraints to social integration generally have not given sufficient concern to subtleties in the changing meanings and modes of social integration; (3) Measures of social integration have focused on the presence or absence of any number of activities and have not attended to the processual aspects of social life.

SOCIAL INTEGRATION AS PROBLEMATIC

One way of addressing and understanding the matter of social integration is to become reflexive and ask questions about the research act, the interpretation of empirical materials, and the implications of analysis. In effect, social integration must be made "problematic." It must become a puzzle to be solved rather than something found in the empirical world. If the matter of social integration becomes a puzzle, it becomes a problem to be solved with some difficulty and through ingenuity. The implication is that a broad range of techniques, approaches, sources, and styles of thought must be brought into play if the entire picture is to be pieced together. Of course, the first step toward finding the solution to a puzzle is that of making sure the necessary pieces are present. Thus, if the study of social integration is to become a problematic enterprise, a few basic questions are in order. These simple but not so obvious questions are intended to focus attention on some overlooked or taken-for-granted aspects of social integration.

Of Whom?

When a study of social integration is developed, of whom will we have a portrait when it is finished? This question addresses more than the mundane but necessary problems of sampling and selection.

Instead, the intent is to uncover some more subtle problems arising out of inattention to certain qualities and characteristics of the aged being studied. Consider the example of much research focused on the institutionalized aged. Most of these studies have asked questions about numbers of resources, friends, relatives, and other kinds of support (Atchley, 1980; Hess and Waring, 1978). Important distinctions have been made about whether these factors are found inside or outside institutional walls. These walls, then, became influential determinants of the nature and degree of social integration discovered. It is possible to learn from these studies that giving assistance, receiving attention from others, and participation in social activities are crucial for satisfactory social integration into the nursing home milieu. However, next to nothing is learned about integration in the lives of the aged. Are the Jewish, Black, Asian, Catholic, or Baptist among them linked into the belief and value systems of those concerns? Are there group memberships and social roles that are not impeded by institutional walls? Essentially, studies of this type are not studies of the integration of older people, but of the effects of institutions on aspects of social interaction and well-being.

Therefore, studies of social integration should pay attention to the backgrounds, beliefs, and characteristics of those studied. These factors are important whether the intent is to analyze the social integration of selected older individuals, the inner city aged, minority elderly, residents of retirement communities, the aged in age-mixed neighborhoods, or whomever. So much of the multidimensional character of social integration *and* the aged is lost when the vision of individuals operating in many facets of everyday life is ignored.

Into What Form?

From where do the social roles, group memberships, and social values that constitute social integration arise? To a large degree these links into society originate from and are oriented toward social organizational forms of various kinds. Broadly conceived, it might be said that all groups and relationships have definite forms, structures, and functions. The early sociologist Georg Simmel noted that individuals stand at the intersection of many groups and social organizational forms. The study of social integration, therefore, should pay close attention to the differences among them and the implications they hold for linking the aged into social life. These are important pieces in the puzzle of social integration to be solved.

The most distinctive feature of kinship as a social organizational form, for example, might be the notion of permanent group membership (see Adams, 1968; Litwak and Szelenyi, 1969). There is little choice regarding the content of a kinship group and how long social integration within might last. However, the importance and centrality of this form in the lives of the aged certainly changes over time. Similarly, friendships offer the opportunity for older people to match their status characteristics with others (see Blau, 1961; Hess, 1979; Riley and Foner, 1968). It is the mutual affinity between individuals that holds this form together. Therefore, integration of the aged into friendship dyads or groups may be a tenuous but highly rewarding endeavor. Informal groups, interest groups, territorial communities, voluntary associations, formal organizations, and the like all provide social integration for the aged. Greater attention must be given, then, to the distinctive character of these forms and the ways they are combined in the lives of older people to provide social integration. The effects of the changes and losses that accompany old age differentially affect life in these social organizational forms.

From What State?

When piecing together the puzzle of social integration at a single point in time, it is also important to understand the previous state of the aged. In a general sense, many researchers have acknowledged the roles, values, and memberships of the middle years and noted changes of the cohort as they reached old age. However, a complete sensitivity to previous integrative states of older people would require some knowledge of their earlier lives in various social organizational forms. Through knowledge of the specific routes traveled by the aged to their current state, the underlying functions and meanings of their social integration might be uncovered.

A fine example of addressing such matters is Arlie Russell Hochschild's (1978) study of the retirement community Merrill Court. Knowledge of the midwestern, working-class roots of most residents and their working lives in the steel and shipyards of Northern California had great value in explaining their orientation toward the retirement community. Many of the values, memberships, and roles that provided social integration for them in old age were not spontaneous constructions. Instead, much of the style and substance of their social integration was carried over from earlier states. These are the kinds of subtleties missed in a great many studies of social integration.

Along What Lines?

If the aged are integrated into a variety of social organizational forms, then there must be a broad range of lines that serve as their linkages with others. An explicit awareness of the lines by which the aged are connected with others would demand a focus on the "hows" of social integration. In other words, what are the actions that link people into various forms of social organization and what channels of communication serve as facilitators? An uncovering of those lines and avenues would reveal much about the kinds of experiences the aged will have and the degree of commitment involved. Sociologists and social gerontologists have long emphasized the importance of face-to-face interaction in primary groups (see Babchuk, 1978; Bates and Babchuk, 1961; Dono et al., 1979). The lines of involvement in such groups probably are copresent verbal interaction based on kinship, affinity, neighborhood ties, and so on. What lies underexplored are the many other lines that manage to connect people together. Lyn Lofland, for example, has discussed the idea of "dispersed villages" created by strategic use of the automobile (1973: 136). Modern urbanites sometimes manage to piece together and connect their places of residence, work, shopping, visitation, and the like. All of these places may be separated by vast distances and spaces, but the automobile facilitates the connection of these places into an understandable whole without the drivers ever stepping foot into the alien neighborhoods, suburbs, and city spaces through which they must pass. The meaning and function of automobiles, recreational vehicles, mobile homes, rental condominiums, ocean cruises, and so on for the aged represent lines of connection. These are, in addition to mass communications, extremely important for linking the aged with others.

To What End?

Integration into society involves actions of many kinds serving a wide variety of functions, purposes, and ends. Therefore, a complete understanding of aged involvement in various forms of social organization also implies knowledge of what the older people themselves derive from them. This question focuses not so much on matters of personal meaning, but on the instrumental and expressive ends achieved. Do the aged make money through their endeavors? Are the functions those of receiving or administering support of various kinds? Is it a pleasurable activity requiring substantial economic investment? Do the integrative experiences provide the aged with opportunities for nurturance and feelings of self worth (see Weiss, 1969)?

The distinction between work and leisure is an artificial one that glosses over the interrelated nature of instrumental and expressive ends. For example, Edwin Christ's (1965) study of retired stamp collectors highlighted the economic functions of what is ostensibly a leisure activity. In addition, the older stamp collectors occasionally relocated to cities known for widespread philatelic activity. Inevitably, there were friendships and other primary relationships evolving out of what began as an activity focused toward different ends. Therefore, the ends achieved by the aged in any number of social involvements and relationships may be in constant process. In illustration, it was not unusual to find older women who had turned their love of knitting or needlepoint into hobbies that eventually expanded into small, part-time businesses.

With What Meaning?

Finally, the role of specific integrative experiences in supplying personal meaning to the aged demands attention. How do specific involvements serve as sources of personal identity, self-concept, and feelings of social value? To explain further, the aged tend to develop a number of personal identities revolving around their involvements in senior centers, retirement communities, sewing circles, country clubs, fraternal orders, churches, and so on. Most important, however, is the idea that people order their personal identities on a hierarchy of prominence, with some more highly valued than others. Those identities created and maintained through great personal effort, sacrifice, or economic expenditure tend to be more highly valued than others (see Heiss, 1981; Stryker, 1968). Therefore, when confronted by losses or limitations of various kinds, the aged often must make decisions regarding the focus of their involvements. These decisions represent strategic actions designed to maintain the more highly valued identities at the expense of others. Knowledge of the decision-making process and the content of the decisions would reveal much about the meaning of certain involvements.

FOCUSING ON SOCIAL WORLDS

With these suggestions and warnings in mind, the focus shifts to the specific form of social organization within which the integration of the aged will be explored. A more detailed discussion of social worlds, their unique characteristics, and how they differ from other social organizational forms will facilitate understanding of the role and place of the aged within them. While a focus on social worlds will not clarify all aspects of social integration in old age, it will set the context for the analysis of aging lives to follow.

In the following pages, the social world is contrasted with five well-known organizational forms. While distinct norms, values, status hierarchies, and the like arise in all social organizational forms, it is important to focus on that which is distinctive about social worlds and personal involvement. Eight features have been selected that highlight some crucial differences about social worlds and bring these matters to the forefront of consciousness. The value of Figure 1.1, beyond clarification of social worlds, is the development of portraits of the *informal group, interest group, formal organization, territorial community,* and *voluntary association* as recognizeable forms for comparison. Of course, some of these forms include features characteristic of social worlds, but they do so in smaller proportions, magnitudes, and degrees of importance.

Population Encompassed

Social worlds have the capacity to encompass hundreds or thousands of people within their separate spheres of influence. For example, consider the exceedingly large numbers of people identifying with the worlds of art, stamp collecting, automobile collecting, and music (see Becker, 1982; Christ, 1965; Dannefer, 1980). In essence, the potential population for a social world is limited only insofar as

FORMS OF SOCIAL ORGANIZATION

	Social World	Voluntary Association	Territorial Community	Formal Organization	Interest Group	Informal Group
Population Encompassed	Very Large	Moderate	Moderate	Moderate	Small to Moderate	Small
Dominant Boundary Characteristic	Cognitive Identification	Formal Membership	Spatial Contiguity	Bureaucratic Lines	Cognitive Identification	Spatial Contiguity
Permeability Of Organization Structure	Highly Permeable	Relatively Impermeable	Relatively Impermeable	Relatively Impermeable	Moderately Permeable	Moderately Permeable
Influence Of Authority Structure	Weak	Moderate	Weak	Strong	Moderate	Weak
Rate Of Organization Change	Rapid	Moderate	Slow	Slow	Moderate	Rapid
Basic For Personal Involvement	Shared Perspectives & Interests	Shared Perspectives & Interests	Propinquity	Propinquity & Shared Interests	Shared Perspectives & Interests	Propinquity
Character Of Social Roles	Highly Informal	Moderately Formal	Highly Informal	Highly Formal	Moderately Informal	Informal
Dominant Mode Of Interaction	Use Of Various Media	Face-to-Face & Use Of Media	Face-to-Face	Face-to-Face	Face-to-Face & Use Of Media	Face-to-Face

Figure 1.1: Typology of Social Organizational Forms

information and knowledge about its existence is available or restricted. In other words, anyone who is in the position to hear or read about the activities and processes of a social world is a potential participant.

Unlike the other forms of social organization in Figure 1.1, a social world's population is not restricted by where people are physically located, whether their names appear on membership rosters, or if their involvement is visible to others. What does matter is where their attention is directed and from where personal identity is derived. As Tamotsu Shibutani (1961) noted, social worlds are largely "organized outlooks" created by people in interaction with one another. Any number of communication channels, then, has the potential to facilitate formation of a social world.

These networks of communication are created and maintained through the use of *linking devices*. All social worlds tend to employ newsletters, magazines, bulletins, and telephones to disseminate knowledge about their activities. While it is certainly true that formal organizations, voluntary associations, and interest groups also employ such means, social worlds differ in the degree to which linking devices are vital for organization. Most of the other forms in Figure 1.1 also rely on generous measures of conventional bases for social organization (e.g., formal membership, spatial contiguity, rational-bureaucratic lines, etc.). Therefore, matters of communication and the ability to link actors in ways that transcend space are more crucial for social worlds than for other, more territorial forms.

As a practical consideration, then, no one really knows the number of people identifying with specific social worlds. It certainly is conceiveable that a relatively accurate enumeration of those involved might be achieved through sophisticated procedures, but that is not the concern of this study. For the study of social integration in old age, this notion implies the hidden presence of the aged in a wide variety of social worlds. These are the invisible lives to be explored. Many of those involved have not made their presence or personal interest in various social worlds known to others. In other words, the use of linking devices allows the aged to connect with others sharing interests in such diverse matters as photography, music, needlepoint, art, dance, and bicycling without being visibly involved.

Dominant Boundary Characteristic

In Figure 1.1 the conventional bases that serve as boundaries for other social organizational forms are listed. For example, voluntary associations tend to link people on the basis of membership or formal recognition of involvement. Similarly, bureaucratic lines generally define who is to be considered part of a formal organization (see Blau, 1974; Haas and Drabek, 1973; Hall, 1977), while geographical space serves the same purpose in neighborhoods, housing developments, and other territorial communities (see Poplin, 1979). For social worlds, however, the crucial determinant of boundaries is the cognitive identification of the people involved. If individuals perceive themselves as integrated, are viewed by others as such, or engage in actions that link them into the concerns of a social world, then they are at least marginally integrated.

This guideline does not equally apply to most other forms of social organization. For example, even though voluntary associations may transcend space and link people together, no matter how much they wish to be Masons, Rotarians, PTA members, or whatever, they are not considered such unless formal membership exists. Interest groups, on the other hand, tend to resemble social worlds in the sense that cognitive identification is the dominant boundary characteristic. However, social worlds encompass larger numbers of people and it is more likely that interest groups will formalize through the incorporation of bureaucratic definitions and formal membership requirements (see Freeman, 1975). Therefore, in the study of the aged in social worlds, this feature implies some difficulty in determining when older people are involved and when they are not. While this point will be elaborated later, it is enough at this point simply to note that the self-conceptions and personal identities of the aged themselves will be given more weight than the opinions of others. In short, if the aged believe they are integrated into specific social worlds and engage in actions as if that were true, they will be considered such.

Permeability of Organization Structure

While voluntary associations, territorial communities, and formal organizations may seek to bar entry of some people into their domain by restricting membership or patrolling spatial boundaries, social worlds are able to exert far less control over sources of information and the acquisition of knowledge. Thus, in a comparative sense, the organizational structure of this form is highly permeable. In other words, social actors move rather easily into a social world's sphere of influence simply by tapping into one of the many forms of communication utilized.

With the easy penetration of the organizational structure, people bring with them new ideas, practices, and procedures. Thus, the boundaries of social worlds must be rather elastic and amorphous to compensate for the actors, organizations, events, and practices that are entering and departing. In focusing on social worlds, this continual shifting complicates the matter of determining the values, roles, and evaluation of those within. The continual entry of new ideas and practices means that such matters are in a constant state of flux. For the study of aging lives, continual change implies that older people may be trying to maintain integration in a form which keeps changing and, perhaps, slipping away. Of course, the imagery of constant change also suggests that specific social worlds may experience potentially dramatic fluctuations in numbers of participants. In many ways, the processes of growth and decline found in many social worlds resemble some theoretical treatments of social movements.[3] Therefore, any analysis of older people in social worlds must be grounded in time and place since the proportion, status, and evaluation of the aged may change.

Influence of Authority Structure

In varying degrees, all forms of social organization develop authority structures that formulate policy, disseminate information, make decisions regarding procedure, engage in justifications, and other similar activities (see Mott, 1965). Since social worlds tend to encompass and include voluntary associations, formal organizations, territorial communities, and interest groups, multiple authority structures are present. The presence of these other forms within social worlds implies the existence of pockets of rigidity within an otherwise loose and amorphous system. For example, the art world includes artist associations, regional societies, and schools that compete for resources, recognition, prestige, and domination.

The lack of a single, unified authority structure also means that whatever direct influence a social world has over individuals probably is located in subworlds. All social worlds are reducible to at least several subworlds. Once again, the art world includes subworlds based on region (e.g., the New York, Chicago, or Paris art worlds), media emphasized (e.g., sculpting, painting, photography), orientation (e.g., abstract expressionism, realism, or pop art), or even media (oils, acrylics, watercolors), to name a few.[4]

In focusing on the aged, the matter of subworlds hints at the existence of clusters of older people within various larger social worlds. These subworlds might be organized around shared cohort experiences, historical periods, generational interests, and even fads rooted in their youth. Consider the subworlds in the social world of dance organized around ballroom dancing, big band music, dixieland jazz, and square dancing. The lack of well-defined, strong authority structures also has implications for the location and evaluation of older people in various social worlds. While this point will later be explored in detail, it is enough here to note the general lack of control in most social worlds over retirement and other age-related restrictions. When such controls are exerted, they likely arise in one of the formal organizations or voluntary associations located within.

Rate of Organization Change

While important changes in content or focus in voluntary associations, formal organizations, or interest groups may have to be introduced formally and approved among the membership, such is not the case in social worlds. Rather, change tends to be a more spontaneous occurrence than in some other forms. To extend the comparison further, territorial communities face quite another problem. To alter the spatial parameters of a neighborhood or business district requires that a great many people explicitly acknowledge and accept the changes. In this way, changes in the allocation of resources within a territory tend to be negotiated and debated among competing interests in face-to-face meetings.

Changes in a social world, on the other hand, tend to be undertaken rapidly and incorporated. Absence of a strong central authority structure and rigid bureaucracy is conducive to rapid social change. The presence of numerous competing interests in such a loosely organized network of people facilitates and induces rapid alterations in direction, content, and tone. In a sense, this form of social organization exemplifies much of that which characterizes modern social life. The mind-boggling introduction of ideas and technologies requires a form of social organization capable of impulsive alterations. Social worlds and their subworlds are perhaps able to respond to dramatic changes in products, procedures, marketing, ideas, technology, numbers of participants, and social trends more rapidly than other forms.

When focusing on older participants, it is important to acknowledge this tendency toward change. The kinds of knowledge that once facilitated integration into certain social worlds may rapidly be replaced. People with outdated knowledge may find themselves excluded from certain circles, or relegated to lesser forms of involvement than they once might have had. Consider the older person trying to reenter the world of ham radio after a layoff of several decades, or even several years. While the act of conducting a ham radio broadcast may not have changed, the electronics involved and the repair procedures may be quite different.

Basis for Personal Involvement

People become integrated into various forms of social organization for a wide variety of reasons, motivations, functions, and rewards. The notion of abstract bases for personal involvement taps the primary factor that draws people into each of the forms in Figure 1.1. If cognitive identification is the dominant boundary characteristic of social worlds, then it is important to uncover the underlying basis for its existence. In other words, cognitive identification is the result of continued exposure to the ideas, practices, procedures, and concerns of a particular social world. The basis for personal involvement, then, addresses the precondition for the cognitive identification that may later arise.

People have varied interests and perspectives bringing them into contact with others sharing similar interests. Eventually, some of them will identify with a specific social world organized around those interests. For example, a mild interest in the stamps of different countries or periods is not enough to link people meaningfully into the stamp collecting world. Instead, it is knowledge of the values, classifications, origins, dealers, and markets of stamps shared with others that begins to link them into this social world. Of course, the matter of sharing and comparing this knowledge with others need not be face-to-face nor even directed toward specific people. Once again, the value of newsletters, magazines, and books, cannot be overemphasized in this regard. Therefore, shared interests and perspectives must exist before cognitive identification with a specific social world is achieved.

Character of Social Roles

Forms of social organization might further be distinguished by noting the character of social roles. While all forms include a combination of formal and informal roles, there are tendencies toward one or the other. The portraits sketched in Figure 1.1 convey a great deal about the character of social roles within these forms. In social worlds, people may move in and out with relative ease. The implication of the previous organizational characteristics is that social roles are necessarily informal. The notion of amorphous boundaries coupled with weak authority structures means that people are not directly controlled, nor do they tend to follow prescribed routes of integration. Of course, some formal roles exist in social worlds. However, they are likely to arise in the many voluntary associations, formal organizations, and interest groups situated within larger worlds. For example, professional and business associations within the art world may have executive officers, representatives, lobbyists, and managers. However, the people who occupy such roles represent a very small proportion of the total population of social world participants. The degree to which roles in social worlds may take on an informal quality is exemplified by the fact that people may identify with the concerns of a social world and may not be acknowledged by others. The use of linking devices allows people to form connections outside the vision of others.

Dominant Mode of Interaction

Finally social worlds rely upon various media to link those who identify with their concerns. Therefore, largely because of the spatially transcendant character of this form of social organization, interaction via the media is the dominant mode. This is the only way an extremely large number of spatially dispersed people could be meaningfully linked. Of course, face-to-face interaction among social world participants routinely occurs. For example, social worlds of many kinds organize auctions, conventions, meets, and exhibits where participants may meet one another. Yet, most of the everyday activities that keep particular social worlds functioning are accomplished via the media.

Of the other forms of social organization portrayed in Figure 1.1, interest groups and voluntary associations seem most dependent upon media of various kinds. Voluntary associations usually have local and regional chapters that must be linked. Similarly, interest groups may be concentrated in particular areas of the country even though many participants are dispersed throughout the nation. For example, many lobbying bodies or political action groups are concentrated in Washington, D.C. or New York, yet the bulk of their membership must be linked through the media. Of course, the more densely situated groups are in geographical space, the more likely face-to-face interaction will be the dominant mode.

THE RESEARCH PROCESS

Throughout this chapter an approach toward social integration in old age and the relevance of social worlds has been developed. The essence of the argument is that a focus on the aged in social worlds will lead to a more complete portrait of social life in the later years than currently exists in sociology and social gerontology. The next order of business is a discussion of the research process by which the social lives of selected older people were uncovered, explored, and analyzed. Therefore, in the following pages particular attention will be given to the selection of older individuals for the interviews, the direction of the interviews themselves, and the process of analyzing and working with the empirical materials that arose.

The Fieldwork

The most feasible strategy for exploring the relevance of social world involvement in the lives of older people and the broader issue of social integration was the focused but unstructured interview (see

Lofland, 1971, 1976). This format facilitates the pursuit of a broad range of relevant issues, while having the flexibility to seize upon an emergent topic and pursue it with some depth. Consequently, the range and extent of many social involvements could be explored, as well as an in-depth examination of integration into social worlds.

With the specific focus of the aged and social worlds in mind, the interviewing process was begun. Forty older people living in Northern California were interviewed over a two year period. All lived in the region surrounding Sacramento, the state capitol, and within an hour's drive of San Francisco and the Bay Area. Location near several cities and a university community tended to bring ideas, activities, and involvements to the aged that might not have been available to others in more isolated areas. This geographical area was perceived to be a theoretically rewarding site because of the many social worlds apparent in urbanized society (see Fischer, 1982). One other point must be made. The fact that many of the older people lived in a suburban area, which had retained some aspects of the small town it once was, meant that their lives often contained a mix of urban and small town associations.

All of the interviews were tape recorded and eventually transcribed for analysis. Everyone involved was assured of privacy and confidentiality. From the beginning, they were told that pseudonyms would be created to replace real names, and that identities would be obscured as much as possible — hopefully without destroying the character or quality of their lives. No one expressed much concern over the matter and, in fact, many seemed to wish their identities might not be obscured. Apparently, some older people felt their lives exemplary and that their stories might help others age successfully. Of course, there were several others who relished the attention and sought a modicum of recognition and publicity. Only once did any of the older people contacted for an interview refuse. In this instance, the woman had been interviewed for another university project and simply assumed she had already contributed to the study. In other instances, however, the initial telephone conversation to arrange the interview required statements convincing the aged that participation was important. Those older people who expressed hesitancy did not seem to do so out of suspicion or cynicism, but rather because they viewed themselves as ordinary and their lives mundane. When informed that such probably was not the case, but that if it were true that this too would be relevant, consent followed. Of course, not all interviews were as rewarding and informative as others, but all proved valuable for the integration they revealed and the limitations uncovered.

The first several people to be interviewed were selected not for their random qualities as typical representatives of the aged, but because they were believed to be involved in social worlds. The list from which the theoretical sample was drawn consisted of names found in local newspapers, referrals by friends, suggestions by their relatives and prominent older people in the community (see Glaser and Strauss, 1967). The first of those contacted also provided names and leads that supplemented the list of possible older people to interview.

The introductory interviews, of one to two hours in length, were used to identify the importance and centrality of social worlds in certain aging lives. To facilitate this, a broad range of questions were asked concerning the nature of activities, concerns, and involvements. The ambiguity of deciding whether or not an activity constituted involvement in a social world was reduced by employing the notion "breadth of perspective" (see Warshay, 1962). For example, the activity of bowling arose in several interviews. For one older woman, bowling was a means to meet available men, create friendships, and stay active. This woman did not know nor care much about bowling itself. Largely unaware of professional associations, local clubs, and tournaments, bowling for her was an excuse for informal group activity. For another couple, however, bowling was a major focus of their lives. They engaged in the activity three or four times a week and constantly talked about it. When traveling along the West Coast to visit children, they attended professional tournaments and knew that senior citizen leagues existed everywhere. They used this knowledge to meet people sharing their ages and interests. Therefore, for the latter couple, bowling constituted a social world involvement.

Experience and perception gained in the first dozen interviews allowed greater depth to the focus on social worlds and their role in the lives of the aged. The kinds of verbal evidence likely to lead to discovering involvement in social worlds was more readily apparent. Therefore, this phase of roughly twenty interviews with older people, ranging in age from 62 to 85, allowed the theoretical exploration of aging lives in various arrangements related to housing, economics, physical condition, and family status. These are the people who appear in the study as major characters, providing life histories and illustrative material.

Building upon information gathered, it was also possible to identify some social worlds that encourage, discourage, or remain indifferent to older participants. Therefore, a portion of those interviewed were selected because they provided in-depth knowledge of specific worlds. In most instances these were people involved in several social worlds, which arose during earlier conversations. For example, an early interview uncovered an elaborate network of ballroom dancers in the Sacramento area. Several older people were then chosen for interviews specifically because they were also ballroom dancers. In this way greater understanding of the role of the aged in certain social worlds was gained. Portraits of selected social worlds will later be elaborated.

The final set of approximately eight interviews was used to fill gaps in information and pursue certain issues and ideas with somewhat greater depth. Several people contacted during this period did not qualify as older people, but as representatives of specific social worlds in which several major characters in the study were involved. This was an attempt to confirm the perceptions of the older participants, or acquire an entirely different view on the matter of aged integration.

Finally, it should be noted that the interviewing process included a subtle element of fieldwork and observation. Nearly all interviews occurred in the homes of older people. This allowed observation of the home base from which social integration activities originated. It was possible to get a rudimentary impression of the character of their lives, as well as discovering topics of conversation that might otherwise have been overlooked. For example, most homes are storehouses of mementos, artifacts, and objects that symbolize social involvements of the present and the past. When interviewed, some older people referred to these objects and used them to stimulate memories of the past.[5] The objects and arrangements of their homes also provided focus to interview questions that might have seemed out of place in other contexts. Photographs of families, for example, provided a way of asking questions about spouses, children, grandchildren, and relationships without appearing intrusive.

Profiles of Social Involvement

Fourteen individuals emerged out of the interviews as major characters whose lives best illustrate the range, diversity, and influence of many factors on integration of the aged in social worlds. Throughout this study the lives of these people will be introduced and analyzed as vehicles by which social integration may be understood and explained in both theoretical and practical terms.

To encapsulize rather complex social lives, profiles of social involvement have been constructed. These profiles are intended to capture and portray most of the involvements that provided integration into society for the aged individuals. Whenever possible, the specific form of social organization toward which these activities and involvements were directed have been identified, categorized, and portrayed. In this way a better understanding of the linkages that bind the older people with others might be conveyed.

A few words must be said about converting interview material into profiles of social involvement. Throughout the interviews much attention was directed not only at the discovery of integration, but also toward the focus of activity in various forms of social organization. Therefore, in addition to identifying social world activities, attempts were made to classify involvement in voluntary associations, formal organizations, interest groups, territorial communities, families, and the like. Of course, while detailed portraits of aged integration are constructed, they do not capture the entire picture. For example, integration into society through social values formed in the past are not likely to be tapped, nor are certain interpersonal relations and friendships. Instead, it is argued that the profiles capture the social integration that lies at the forefront of consciousness among the older people. These are matters that seem to be on their minds and can be expressed verbally.

To illustrate the process of profile construction, consider the case of Arnold and Jean Goodrich. At the ages of 68 and 63, this older couple identified a broad range of social involvements. For example, their children lived within an hour's drive and they have maintained close contact over the years. In fact, at the time of the interviewing, one son was living with them until he could find a suitable apartment. They lived in a mobile home park largely populated by older people and college students. Within this residential area they developed a number of strong friendships and regularly met with other residents as an acting body to formulate policy, do repairs, and socialize.

As a couple, Arnold and Jean had become well-integrated into the social world of bowling. As earlier described, they regularly bowled three or four times weekly, used the activity to meet others, and attended professional tournaments. In this involvement the couple continued to perform the activities more or less together and seemed equally integrated. However, such was not the case with all social activities and involvements. Jean was a member of an informal bridge group that met weekly and included several close friends. Arnold did not have any desire or interest in the activity. The problem of separating individual from couple-based involvements during a joint interview was a difficult, but not insurmountable task. For the most part, the degree of verbal contribution seemed to indicate the personal meaning to individuals. Those who demonstrated more in-depth knowledge about a social world than the other, for example, agreed they were more deeply integrated. However, attempts were made to gain both perspectives on involvement by contrasting responses to similar questions. Of course, different constructions of reality existed and care had to be taken to define whose version was being reported. Most involvements seemed to be noncontroversial between members of the couples.

A final point must be made about the processual nature of social life and how it is reflected in the profiles. The profiles can only represent the social lives of older people as they were conveyed at the time of the interviews. Even then, many of their lives were changing. The Goodrichs previously had traveled extensively, using their travels both to create new friendships and renew old ones. Due to inflation and life on a fixed income, they were cutting back on traveling when interviewed. Conversely, they had begun to visit the local senior center and considered it a joint venture, even though each engaged in quite different activities once they were there. Arnold volunteered for repair work and clean-up duties, while Jean was involved in quilting and dance groups. Therefore, the following symbols illustrate the processual and dynamic features of social integration in the profiles: stable (_____), entering (. . . . .), and withdrawing (--------).

When social lives are as segmented as those of Arnold and Jean Goodrich, it is difficult to rank their social involvements in order of

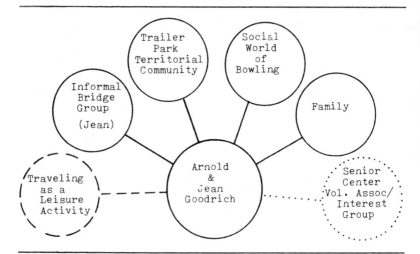

Figure 1.2: Profile of Arnold and Jean Goodrich

importance. It is clear that each involvement had a meaning and function different from the others. Therefore, it is perhaps more useful to analyze the degree to which lives of the aged were segmented, the meanings of various involvements, and the social integration that emerged out of the sum total of their immersion in social life. The most pressing issue at hand concerns the role of social worlds in aging lives.

NOTES

1. While studies of social integration make up a significant proportion of the total content in social gerontology, few researchers explicitly locate their research into this body of knowledge. Specifically, studies focusing on a wide variety of issues have matters of social integration at their base. The most widely known are those studies of retirement communities (Aldridge, 1959; Hochschild, 1973; Hoyt, 1954; Jacobs, 1974; Johnson, 1971; Kleemeier, 1954; Marshall, 1973, 1975), voluntary associations (see Babchuk and Booth, 1969; Smith, 1966; Trela, 1972; Wright and Hyman, 1958), interest groups (Jacobs and Hess, 1978; Pratt, 1974; 1976; Riemer and Binstock, 1978), and senior centers (Carp, 1976; Hanssen et al., 1978; Trela, 1971). Somewhat less obvious among studies of this type are those of certain aspects of

family life (Shanas et al., 1968), nursing home experiences (Gubrium, 1975), inner city support systems (Cantor, 1975), and other miscellaneous social involvements (see Taietz and Larson, 1956; Streib and Streib, 1975).

2. A major exception to the generalization that older people do not develop strong commitment to groups and friendships formed in old age lies in the work of Jeffrey Rosenfeld (1979, 1980). In his study of the wills and bequeaths of older people, Rosenfeld discovered a number of people who created intense and meaningful relationships among those in nursing homes, retirement communities, and homes for the aged. In fact, some older people changed their wills to bequeath much of their wealth to fellow residents or the institution at the expense of other heirs.

3. In the process of analyzing the growth and decline of a specific social world (the world of surfing), John Irwin devised a scheme of phases relevant to the study of social worlds in general (1977). The phases Irwin employed were: *formation, expansion, corruption,* and *decline.* Upon close scrutiny, it is apparent that these phases closely correspond to the stages through which crazes, fads, and fashions are also said to pass (Berk, 1974; Penrose, 1952; Turner and Killian, 1972). The *formation phase* marks the point at which a small group of individuals begins to focus on a particular social object. It is at this time that a core of people, who derive major portions of their identity from surfing, bicycling, or dancing, begin to congregate and disseminate knowledge of their interests through social networks. Recruitment often assumes the nature of "whirlpools," wherein the core draws others into the sphere (see Crane, 1972; Griffiths, 1939). Of course, there are many social worlds that passed through this phase so long ago that the notion loses meaning. For example, the social worlds of art, science, dance, and music have existed for many years. The *expansion phase* captures the growth that takes place after knowledge about the activity has been disseminated. At this time, core members tend to lose control of that which originally bound them. The exponential growth usually is the result of the personal influence process and is facilitated by word of mouth (see Rogers, 1962). Publicity in mass media also contributes to diffusion and it is inevitable that competing ideologies and orientations will develop. During the *corruption phase,* large numbers of people become involved in a social world and it is signified when the founding group loses control of the many actors, organizations, events, and practices devised. In Irwin's words, the ideology is mangled by large numbers of participants. In the world of surfing, Irwin saw that word of dissatisfaction among original members spread to the outlying sources of newcomers, halted them from joining the scene, and growth ceased (1977: 150). Therefore, the *stagnation phase* is the fourth stage at which the social world has neither the vitality nor spirit that marked earlier phases. Participants may begin to defect and the many organizations, events, and practices that evolved may begin to fade away. Of course, not all social worlds reach this phase but may, instead, experience the previous stages in cyclical fashion.

4. The matter of subworlds demands greater explanation regarding their formation. Rob Kling and Elihu Gerson (1978) have analyzed how subworlds of the larger computing world are generated by (1) kinds of problems to be solved, (2) kinds of technology used, (3) varieties of application, and (4) relationship to IBM. The process out of which subworlds develop is segmentation, or the pervasive tendency for worlds to develop specialized concerns and interests within the larger community

of common activities (Kling and Gerson, 1978: 26; Strauss, 1978a). Subworld formation may be due to a combination of several factors, but at least six sources of
segmentation may be identified. A shared region occasionally facilitates a common
orientation and perspective. Thus, *space* and the concentration of actors, organizations, events, and practices therein is one source. Another source is the different
kinds of *objects* within a social world. For example, in the world of old car collectors,
there are subworlds formed around Model As, Ford Thunderbirds, early roadsters,
and 1920-era Cadillacs (see Dannefer, 1980). The kind of *technology* employed is
another line of cleavage in a social world. The computing world continues to offer the
most obvious examples of this source. Another major source of segmentation is the
matter of personal *ideology*. Disagreements over political issues, aesthetic judgments, or moral controversies may give rise to distinct splinter groups (see Crane,
1972; Freeman, 1975; Price, 1963). Subworlds may also form at the points where
several social worlds *intersect*. For example, the worlds of art and minority groups
often intersect to form subworlds of Black artists, Asian artists, and the like. Finally,
differential *recruitment* of members into social worlds maximizes the probabilities for
new lines of activity (Strauss, 1979a, 1979b, 1982). For example, decisions to recruit
the aged into the worlds of art, music, square dancing, and ballroom dancing may
create points of intersection that previously did not exist.

    5. In another paper (Unruh, 1983) I have argued that the objects and mementos of
older people may become storehouses of personal identities. With the prospect of
impending death, people become more concerned with the meanings of certain
objects, the identities they represent, and the apportionment of them to potential
survivors. On the other hand, those who receive such objects, and survive the death
of the person to whom they were most meaningful, may use the artifacts to structure
reminiscences of the deceased. This is not a way for survivors to work through and
dispense with lingering images of those who preceded them in death, but an indica-
tion of how memories of the dead thrive through social action and accomplishment.

2

SOCIAL WORLDS IN
AGING LIVES

Increasing age brings with it the potential to change the nature of social integration. Matters of retirement, widowhood, declining economic resources, and residential relocation all affect the character of involvement in society. This chapter focuses on a number of social psychological matters regarding the importance of social worlds in the lives of aging people. As the life cycle progresses and old age approaches, it is important to understand changes in social world identification and involvement. For example, changes may occur in the nature and degree to which older people use social worlds to guide and direct their daily live. Similarly, the increasing awareness of impending death, which tends to accompany old age, also affects the personal meaning derived out of various social worlds. As friends and colleagues fade away through illness, relocation, lack of interest, or death, the ties holding older people into particular social worlds may weaken, or perhaps take on new importance. Finally, social world involvements rooted in the past may be kept alive in the later years and continue to provide a measure of personal meaning.

In exploring these matters it is important to relate an intriguing notion about the identification of social actors with social worlds first acknowledged and discussed by Tamotsu Shibutani (1955). In modern societies, people may sometimes use the standards of social worlds in which they are not recognized members and, perhaps, of those in which they have never directly participated. More intriguing, people may also have vicarious interactions and estimate their endeavors from a perspective imputed to people in the past, idealizing some period of history and longing for the good old days, criticizing current events from a standpoint imputed to people long since dead" (Shibutani, 1955: 566). One example of vicarious involvement in a social world rooted in the past is the case of "medievalists" who acquire their perspectives, values, orientations, and meanings solely through books.

Most important for the study of social worlds in aging lives is the idea that social worlds may be meaningful even though they do not exist in any concrete sense. This idea implies the possibility that the aged may structure their expectations, organize their conduct, and derive personal meaning in reference to some social worlds rooted in the past, situated in the present, or occasionally projected into the future. In effect, it is not so important that particular social worlds actually exist, but that people organize their life-rounds, perceptions, and actions as if they were real. This offers a particularly intriguing idea for focusing on certain aspects of older people's social lives. By analyzing the origins of certain personal identities and the social worlds in which they are located, it is possible to better understand the degree to which their lives are rooted in the past, present, and future. Important differences exist among individual older people regarding the direction of their identities located in time. This chapter will first focus on influences of social worlds on the ways the aged remember the past. The value of such involvements and their influence on efforts to organize the present will be the next major topic of discussion. Throughout, some attention also will be given to orientations toward the future and social world involvements there directed.

REMEMBERING THE PAST

With the onset of old age, it perhaps is inevitable that memories and images of the past increase in both frequency and importance. The sheer number of years lived, coupled with multiple role losses in old age, tend to make past experiences and memories a central component of everyday life. As Victor Marshall and others have noted, old age is accompanied by an increasing awareness of finitude, which may alter orientations toward many aspects of life (see Bengtson et al., 1977 Reynolds and Kalish, 1974; Rosen and Neugarten, 1960). The term awareness of finitude, then, refers to the notion that people become increasingly aware of the end of life, acknowledge the possibility of death, and initiate social and psychological preparation for their demise. Marshall (1980: 107) noted that increased awareness of finitude in old age begins the process of binding together self and death. In other words, people who once viewed themselves as living for many years begin to see themselves as dying. Such increased awareness of finitude is stimulated not only by personal illness or declining abilities, but by things like the deaths of friends or relatives, the approach of the age at which their parents died, average life expectancies, and so on. By conceiving the self as mortal or self as dying, older people are faced with the opportunity (or responsibility) of beginning the social and psychological tasks of making sense of their lives. In Marshall's terms, aging people "come to see themselves in autobiographical perspective. They see the chapters of their lives unfolding, and the heightened awareness of finitude that generally accompanies later life brings them into the last chapter" (1980: 107). The problem for the aged, then, is not one of rewriting the autobiography hidden in their minds so that their lives seem unrealistically successful, happy, or famous. Rather, the process is one of making sense of that which occurred throughout their lives and rendering life meaningful.

This discussion highlights the profound importance that awareness of finitude has on matters of reality construction, self-awareness, and personal meaning in the social lives of the aged (see Havighurst et al., 1968; Tolor and Murphy, 1967). For the most part, studies of the ways by which older people engage in the sense-making, to which Marshall alluded, generally have focused on reminiscence. In briefly explaining this concept, the stage shall further be set for analysis of how the aged reminisce, reinterpret, and hold on to social worlds rooted in the past.

Prior to 1970 the gerontological literature contained few references to reminiscence, with the two most prominent approaches being those of Erik Erikson (1950) and Robert Butler (1963). Subsequent years have yielded much empirically based research, but little consensus regarding the definition, value, and evidence of reminiscence (see Merriam, 1980). For example, the concept variously has been defined as a dwelling on the past, the remembered past, the act of recalling the past, or retrospection both purposive and spontaneous (see Butler, 1970, 1980; Havighurst and Glasser, 1972; Lieberman and Falk, 1971; McMahon and Rhudick, 1967; Merriam, 1980). Regardless of definition and orientation, most researchers have been intent on separating the normal from the pathological, or correlating self-reported reminiscenses of the aged with satisfactory adjustment to the traumas of old age.

In his analysis of nostalgia and the life cycle, Fred Davis offered an approach and attitude relevant to the study of social worlds in aging lives. Even though his attention was on nostalgia rather than the larger issue of reminiscence, it is important to remember that it fulfills the same function for the elderly as it does for younger people. The "chief aim is to assuage the uncertainties and identity threats engendered by problematic life transitions" (Davis, 1979: 69). Thus, there is no reason based on empirical evidence to believe that the aged are less successful in this than others whose lives are similarly mixed up. However, Davis noted that the elderly tend to assimilate matters of reminiscence and self-assessment into the very fabric of their lives. For younger people trying to resolve problematic life situations, these concerns tend to be transient and episodic. Therefore, cognitive ties to the past sustained through reminiscence are crucial components of aging lives.

The extent to which many older people dwelled upon the past during the interviews came as a surprise despite forewarnings implied by research on reminiscence. Throughout the unstructured interviews, a number of people would answer questions about current social activities by first explaining their situation. This meant that they must locate their contemporary social lives within a larger historical and biographical context. Accounts of everyday life were begun by tracing back to the times they entered the work force, married, divorced, became ill, had children, were widowed, and the like. Personal crises and important life events often served as benchmarks for the formation or dissolution of specific social world involvements.

The following section begins the analysis of relatively unstructured reminiscences among the aged. Particular attention is given to

he implicit ways they reminisced, recollected, and reconstructed the
social worlds in which they once were active. Attention will then shift
o the more explicit, formal, and conscious procedures used by cer-
ain older people who actively sought to reconstruct and preserve
cognitive ties to social worlds rooted in the past. In these ways,
artifacts and memories of the past were imbued with meaning so as to
preserve identities built up over many years.

Unstructured Recollections

A great many recollections of the aged seemed to arise in rather
unpredictable and spontaneous ways. The occurrence of these
memories and ties to the past was highly situational. That is, the times
and places where older people found themselves immersed in the past
largely appeared to be out of their direct influence and control. In
conversation, for example, topics arose that spontaneously evoked
memories of previous relationships, activities, or social involvements. These recollections, then, were unstructured in the sense that
older people did not consciously preserve certain memories, attempt
to predetermine their content, and willfully evoke them. Therefore,
when compared to the more highly structured recollections later to be
discussed, it might be said that the unstructured recollections make
up a larger proportion of ties to the past by the aged.

In varying degrees the lives of older people were permeated by
unstructured recollections. Much of the variation had to do with
frequency and intensity of current social involvements, the presence
of active interpersonal relationships, and differences in family situations occurring over time. Almost without exception, the older people whose lives were marked by extensive unstructured recollections
of past social involvements were those who lived in relative isolation,
found themselves alone for significant periods of time, and had an
overwhelming proportion of present social involvements revolving
around the family. In terms of social integration, then, the family may
be the most stable of social organizational forms into which the aged
are integrated. Family membership is not dependant upon physical
abilities, economic resources, residential area, and the like. Of
course, the nature of the family unit changes over the life cycle, but
membership is assumed, stable, durable, and perhaps obligatory (see

Dono et al., 1979). The focus of many recollections, whether highly structured or unstructured, is on family relationships through the years.

Less apparent were those recollections focused on, or derived out of past involvements in other forms of social organization. Personal identities created through participation in social worlds rooted in the past may live on and become the focus of unstructured recollections. The life and recollections of John Weston, a major figure in this study, will better illustrate the role of past social world involvements in the everyday lives of the aged. His life included many qualities and situations that were common to the lives of many older people.

EXAMPLE: JOHN WESTON

At the age of 78, John Weston had been a widower for five years. He had moved to Northern California from Santa Barbara so that he would be near his married daughter and her family. Perhaps more than any other social organizational form, the family had become the central focus of his life. After the death of his wife he reestablished close ties with his family and spent many hours around their house, babysitting, sharing meals, and shopping. He lived for a time with his daughter and her family, but in his words, "seemed to be in the way all the time." His daughter learned of a new housing complex being built for the elderly and managed to reserve a small apartment for him. As a territorial community, the local housing complex began to increase in centrality and importance for John. He personally sought to create a "community" among the residents. The strategies he used were to seek out others, check on the activities of neighbors, try to force others out of their apartments into the courtyard, and to exude friendliness to those who did not seem receptive. As a voluntary association and interest group, the local senior center filled many of John's daytime hours. He spent the better part of most days walking the three-mile round trip between his home and the center. At the time of the interview, he was in the process of becoming integrated into the senior center and the housing complex. These attempts to become reintegrated into certain corners of society came on the heels of a substantial period of loneliness following his wife's death. During that period the family was nearly the only source of integration apparent to others.

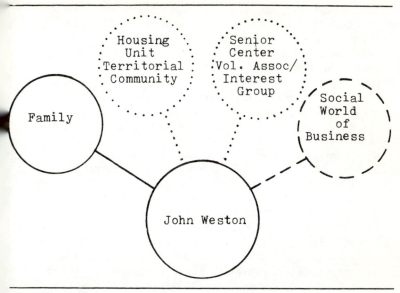

Figure 2.1: Profile of John Weston

The social world of business, however, was the source and location of a great many unstructured recollections that arose during the interview. At the outset, John Weston sought to set the stage for remarks about his current social life by presenting a brief life history. It is important to acknowledge the degree to which his perspective of the past was rooted in one particular social world. While he occasionally referred to various informal groups, voluntary associations, or formal organizations, his was a perspective much broader than that captured by these conventional forms.

In the following interview excerpt, it is possible to see that he did not simply see himself as a former liquor store owner, mâitre d' hôtel, or salesman. Instead, he viewed himself as a survivor of the business world whose many occupations and positions allowed him to understand the workings of this extremely amorphous, vague, and dispersed world. The excerpt begins with a response to questions about the various social activities that currently occupied his time. The extensive biographical life review, which followed slowly and methodically, brought him to the present.

First, I want to tell you that my name is John A. Weston. I was born in Austria-Hungaria, after 1919 it was split up. . . . After 1918 in the new country, we started to see what we could do by ourselves. We, as a people, were always very industrious. We had big breweries and automobile manufacturing. I started work for the Department . . . I guess you could call it the Ministry of Commerce in Prague. Then in 1933, they sent me to Ireland. There, I was involved in making and marketing a combination of gasoline and alcohol. Ireland had a surplus of potatoes at that time, and they converted some of them to alcohol. . . . So when I was in Ireland, I got a big contract for the wooden poles which would bring electricity to the people in the outlying areas. . . . Then, when the war started in Europe, my wife and I moved to America. After managing a liquor business in Florida for a number of years, I went into the restaurant business. We had a friend who was in the business in New Orleans and he talked us into moving there. I started out as a waiter and then we moved to Los Angeles. There, the owner of the restaurant said, "You're a good waiter, but I want you to be a Captain." This is a position of greater responsibility. I then became a head waiter for a while. You know, my name came to be known in the business and so I got a very good offer from a restaurant in Santa Barbara. We spent 18 years in that area at a very famous restaurant, Sommerset, which doesn't exist anymore. I retired in 1965 and didn't really like it very much. So I got a job in a ladies club in Santa Barbara for about three years. I was just too active and felt like I could still make a contribution. I didn't want to sit around and do nothing. . . . My wife died in 1976 and I moved up here.

Only after a lengthy and intense review of John Weston's interview did the underlying functions, motivations, and intentions of his preoccupation with the past become more apparent. In terms of presenting and managing aspects of personal identity to someone (like an interviewer) whose knowledge of him was limited and of a short range nature, recollections served to remind others there was more to this 78-year-old man than first met the eye. Through unstructured recollections, John managed to exude a great deal of information about his many abilities, talents, roles, and positions rooted in social worlds of the past. This is a crucial point because it is only in this seemingly rambling way that meaningful identities and involvements could be revealed that otherwise might have remained untapped, unexplored, or ignored. Therefore, recollections seem to provide the aged opportunites to impart meaningful information not immediately apparent in their daily lives. Further, it is important to note that John took an extrememly active role in seizing the moment allowing the information to flow out of him before the opportunity could slip away. Even though his recollections were unstructured, they represented the active mind of a man concerned with presenting the best possible face.

The example of John Weston calls attention to the importance of knowing the past for truly understanding present circumstances of the aged. John's unstructured recollections, in effect, served as accounts for present circumstances (see Lyman and Scott, 1968). They also served as indicators that he has stood and, in some senses, continued to stand at points within the business world that supplied him with some measure of personal meaning.

The example of John Weston is especially noteworthy because of the degree to which his recollections were rooted in involvements of the distant past. To some degree, this pattern describes most interviews with people in their late 70s and 80s. Those older people focusing on the recent past tended to be younger and more active than John Weston and his cohorts. It might be argued that John and his peers had gradually lost their positions of value in society over the years and, consequently, they became peripheral to many social worlds (see Cumming and Henry, 1961; Cumming, 1964; Gordon, 1975). Therefore, they had to reach far back into the past to locate social worlds in which they were central actors. Along similar lines, Robert Butler noted that the life review process is prompted by the realization of approaching death, and the inability to maintain one's sense of personal invulnerability (1963: 66). It might further be argued that people in their early 60s and 70s need look only to the recent past to locate social worlds in which they held (or continue to hold) central roles.

One final point should be made about unstructured recollections. Tamotsu Shibutani's (1955) claim that social worlds may have personal meaning even though they no longer exist in a concrete sense hints at the importance of yesteryear. Remnants of social worlds and days gone by have provided a kind of satisfaction and contentment for the aged. This especially is true if their every-day lives were marked by depression, loneliness, or isolation. Many of the older women interviewed continued to derive major portions of identity from social world involvements in which they were no longer engaged. For example, two elderly women who had been avid ballroom dancers for many years continued to see themselves as such even though each had stopped dancing for various reasons. Thoughts and attachments to their dancing days served slightly to ease the transition into a less active life. Additionally, some widows continued to derive measures of identity out of social worlds in which their now deceased husbands had been involved. Some older women continued to see themselves as the wives of fire chiefs, physicians, and professors long after their husbands were gone.

The musings of the aged about things once done, accomplishments, and connections in the past allowed them to transcend the confines of time, space, and advanced age — if only for a short time. Never mind that the good old days may have been idealized, what matters is the notion that recollections of the past constituted an aspect of social integration in aging lives not clearly visible or understood by outside observers.

Active Reconstruction

The aged also engaged in more explicit and formalized practices by which they reconstructed and preserved the past. This process of active reconstruction did not permeate the lives of as many older people as the more spontaneous, informal recollections. However some of those interviewed actively engaged in a variety of practices designed to piece together, arrange, and preserve memories of social worlds rooted in the past.

The keeping of diaries, scrapbooks, photo albums, and mementos were activities that stored recollection of the past in physical objects. These objects then served as props that stimulated thinking and guided reminiscences about the content of the journals or photographs, or the circumstances under which they were written or taken. All homes of the older people visited for interviews had family, social, and personal artifacts on display. Tours of homes wherein the meaning and importance of these objects were explained seemed to be standard fare for any first-time visitor.

While nearly all older people engaged in these activities, there were variations in the degree to which they were conscious, planned strategies for the active reconstruction of social world involvements of the past. In other words, there were many older people who engaged in these activities without well-articulated rationales. For a smaller number, however, these activites became an integral part of their current activities. In fact, there were several people who began the process of preserving memories of social world activities while they were still very much involved.

One older couple in their mid-70s compiled a number of scrapbooks and photo albums displaying mementos of their years of immersion in the bicycling world. The husband had competed actively in tours, time trials, and other competitions from his early 60s. Because of his age and abilities, he became well-known to serious bicyclists along the West Coast and across the nation.[1] His notoriety was enhanced by the coverage of his activities in bicycling magazines, local newspapers, television news, and by amateur photographers. While his wife was not a bicyclist, she was his strongest supporter and staunchest ally. Together, they redesigned the wet bar area of their mobile home into a gallery of sorts for the display of these mementos of involvement in the bicycling world. Trophies, framed photographs, posters, racing jerseys, and the vest worn during competitions were displayed prominently. The patches acquired during cross-country and European tours were emblazoned onto the vest, making it the equivalent of the well-traveled suitcase plastered with labels from many countries. Most important, however, is the conscious planning that kept activities of the present for future reference. In essence, they believed the best way of accurately remembering the past was to interpret and preserve it when it was fresh in their minds. The following statement by the elderly bicyclist nicely illustrates this point.

> You know, I won't always be as active as I am now. I'm getting up there in years and so it is important for my wife and me to record these good memories and experiences. God forbid, I may get to the point where I start forgetting things, and these things will help me and my children remember these activities.

For the aged who remained active and well-integrated, the process of active reconstruction was oriented toward the future. They tended to be preserving memories of the fairly recent past for future reference — for times when they might not be as well-integrated. For these older people, the process of reconstructing the past by keeping scrapbooks or organizing mementos was not so much a way of reliving the past, as it was an activity undertaken to ensure that the proper memories and recollections would be available at some unknown time in the future.

Of course,there were other ways by which the aged actively recollected and recorded memories of past social worlds and other involvements. The most obvious method was the actual writing of a life history. The anthropologist Barbara Myerhoff (1978) noted the intense interest among elderly Jews of Venice, California in preserving their life histories through tape recordings or diaries. The experiences of Lucy Anderson, a major figure in this study, help illustrate the degree to which developing a life history can render both the present and the past meaningful.

EXAMPLE: LUCY ANDERSON

At the age of 85, Lucy Anderson was a widow whose husband had died forty years earlier. Since his death, much of her social life focused on her six children and many grandchildren. She spent much of those four decades traveling around the country living near each child for several years at a time. The stability of her integration into the family unit was matched only by the commitment she had in the Church of Jesus Christ of Latter Day Saints. Therefore, much of her free time was spent on work in the Mormon Church and related business. She lived alone and, until the age of 82, had been very active in the ballroom dancing world. Ballroom dancing circuits exist in nearly every city, and she used this knowledge when moving to new areas near her children. Dancing, then, had been a major source of social integration until she suffered a broken hip when struck by a passing automobile. These chronic injuries continued to plague her for a number of years.

It is interesting to note the increased intensity of Lucy Anderson's work on her life history following the accident. Since she no longer devoted four to five nights per week to dancing, there was plenty of time for writing and researching. Interestingly, it was also the accident that impressed her with the importance of getting her story down on paper before it was too late. The family and personal history is a

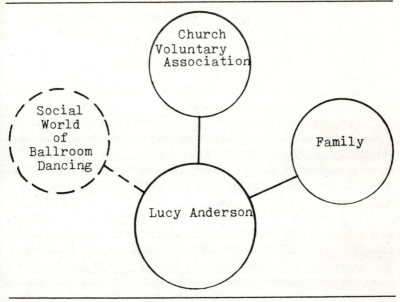

Figure 2.2: Profile of Lucy Anderson

central component of Mormon practice and Lucy wanted hers to be as accurate and up to date as possible. She, therefore, devoted several hours a day literally revising her autobiography. In the following interview excerpt, the relevance of increased awareness of finitude becomes apparent.

> I am now writing my family history since it is a part of the church. I have been involved in the genealogy group there, but now I leave most of that kind of work up to my daughter. I just get too confused sometimes. . . . You know, that picture that came out about that Black family — Roots was its name — that really has gotten a lot of people interested in genealogy. We had a pretty small group of people in our church who were really interested, but after that a number of people from outside the church were interested. I think that is when the group at the senior center got started. . . . I have spent a lot of time on it over the years. Of course, you write your life story as you go along. Now, I am copying it into a permanent book. So I write on it until my eyes get tired. I guess that is usually two or

three hours a day. It is a big project and there are pictures to go with it. I have scads of pictures. . . . Since I'm pretty old by now, I feel like I have to get some of these things down on paper and straightened out. I really don't know if my daughter would know all the details if something happened.

It is apparent that writing the life story not only preserved and communicated much of that which was meaningful about the life of Lucy Anderson, but it supplied her daily life with focus and meaning. The methods necessary for reconstructing her historical family also brought Lucy into contact with the genealogical world. However, it is a world with which she no longer identified even though the procedures she learned and the sourcebooks compiled by genealogists were useful in her work for the church.

The importance of the genealogical world for the lives of many older people should not be overlooked. Courses on methods of reconstructing family histories are taught in senior centers, fraternal associations, and community centers. This is a social world that has blossomed around the felt need of the aged to actively reconstruct histories, memories, and involvements of the past.

ORGANIZING THE PRESENT

Older people are in the constant process of withdrawing out of certain social involvements, discarding obligations, and moving in the direction of new activities. Therefore, the role of social worlds in aging lives changes over time. This is not to say that the lives of the aged are in a constant state of instability, but that several factors work in the direction of change. In addition to changes in circumstances and resources of the aged, the social worlds in which they are integrated are constantly changing. Therefore, the matter of retaining stable and constant integration requires much movement and adaptation on the part of aging individuals.

Often, older people must work very hard at maintaining meaningful involvement in a social world. This form of social organization is not something into which people are born, nor is it part of their neighborhood or city. Instead, the aged must consciously and forthrightly enter a network of communication, establish linkages with others, maintain shared interests, and keep abreast of inevitable changes in that world. Stable integration for the aged is compounded by several factors. First, the activities which once provided integration may be difficult to maintain with increasing age. Matters of forced retirement, physical disability, decreased stamina, loss of a spouse, and other factors may pull people out of certain activities. Second, increasing age may make the aging a minority within worlds dominated by younger people. Even though all social worlds include participants of many ages, marked differences exist regarding proportions of the aged. Changes in these proportions portend difficulties for older people trying to maintain stability. For example, styles and trends favoring younger people may make the contributions of the aged seem obsolete. The dance steps, painting techniques, business knowledge, or other skills offered by older participants may seem to be rooted in the past to those much younger. Therefore, the evaluation of their contribution might diminish. Finally, certain social worlds may actually fragment or dissolve as key leaders grow older. Aging individuals often hold leadership positions in worlds or subworlds. The loss of older leaders may affect the role, evaluation, and experiences of other aging participants. Further, absence of older role models may discourage other aging individuals from becoming involved.

In the following pages the role of social worlds in aging lives is examined by focusing on three processes. The first involves the problem of maintaining enduring integration into certain worlds through the life cycle. Second, aging brings new demands and contingencies that result in people abandoning old involvements. Finally, the process of seeking new social worlds may be an attempt to satisfy new circumstances.

Maintaining Enduring Worlds

There were some older peole who remained integrated into social worlds (and other social organizational forms) throughout most of their lives. In the interviews, several people emerged whose talents, interests, and desires had not changed much over the years. Consequently, some involvements satisfying in the past remained instrumental and vital to their lives in old age. This was the case with several ballroom dancers, auto racing enthusiasts, and artists. Some retired stamp collectors described by Edwin Christ (1965), for example, had been involved most of their lives. Upon retirement, integration in the philatelic world increased in importance. Many aging collectors devoted large amounts of time and resources to collecting, trading, dealing, and selling stamps.

Even though integration may endure over the years, it is likely that orientation toward specific worlds would change throughout the careers of the aged. Therefore, it is necessary to explore the factors which facilitate continued interest in some worlds throughout aging lives. Also, reasons why some involvements endure through the life cycle while others do not must be given attention. Like all social actors, aging people are integrated into social worlds because they share interests with other participants. An important distinction should be made between those whose existing interests bring them into a social world and those who initially are tied through interpersonal relationships. These are not mutually exclusive orientations, but they suggest two distinct reasons for integration into social worlds.

The seven elderly dancers interviewed initially entered the worlds of ballroom and square dancing because of their love for dancing, not due to relationships with specific people. These people were attracted to the activities of these worlds because they had enjoyed dancing most of their lives. Other aging people were attracted to specific worlds through a love of bicycling, the thrill of auto racing, a desire for high-quality foodstuffs, skill at bowling, and interest in business dealings. For many of these people, their integration transcended the influence of specific others. In effect, they remained integrated while the faces around them changed. Individuals had come and gone, but the interests and talents of these people in the activities of certain social worlds remained constant. For example, Lucy Anderson (Figure 2.2.) recited a lengthy list of ballroom dancing circuits in many cities around the country. She was able to find able, knowledgeable, and interested dance partners without the need for close personal relationships. Similarly, knowledge of the rules and procedures allowed aging people to reestablish enduring integration after layoffs of various kinds. An aging square dancer, removed from this world by a heart ailment, sought to return and become reintegrated. In the interview, he described the problem of confronting new square dancing calls, procedures, and methods popularized during his absence.

> Oh, sometimes they have new calls that we haven't heard before. But the new calls are always . . . at least almost always just several old calls arranged together, or strung together in a new way. It takes a while sometimes to get back into the swing of things, but not usually very long. One thing though, you have to be thinking on your feet all the time. . . . Once in a while, they will slip a new call past me and I get confused. That doesn't happen very often. . . .

In this example, the square dancing world had a well-established and respected tradition of calls, routines, and steps. Innovation tended to be bound by this tradition. Similar processes seemed to be operating in the ballroom dancing, bicycling, bowling, and gleaning worlds in which many of the major characters in this study had long been integrated. [2]

On the other hand, when social world activities were secondary to personal relationships, meaningful integration probably did not continue through the life cycle. The people who provided initial linkages for older people probably disappeared or were lost through lack of interest, relocation, disability, or death. A colleague of Lucy Anderson in the ballroom dancing world was involved not through a love for dancing, but to find a suitable marriage partner. This woman did not find what she sought, and eventually stopped dancing altogether. In a sense, it was the inability to create close personal relationships transcending dancing that led to her withdrawal from this world.

EXAMPLE: ROBERT AND SARAH PETERSON

The lives of several major characters in this study illustrate some difficulties in maintaining integration in a social world when linkages are based on personal relationships rather than activities. At the ages of 86 and 84, Robert and Sarah Peterson moved to Northern California to be near their daughter and her family. The family had become important to them in later years, and they moved from Arizona for that purpose. The move removed them from active involvement in the

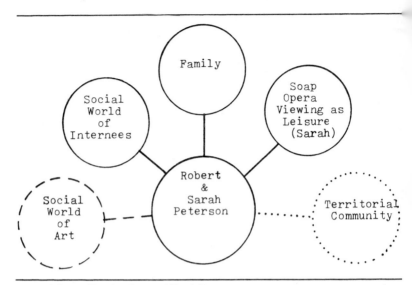

Figure 2.3: Profile of Robert and Sarah Peterson

Phoenix art world. Robert and Sarah had been on executive committees and volunteered their time at local museums. After the move, they remained integrated into the art world only through television and art journals. The neighborhood in which they lived was of marginal importance, although they had attended a block party just before the interview. At that time, they believed themselves more integrated into that territorial community.

In this context it is important to speak about their involvement in a social world of internees. During the 1920s and 1930s, Robert was a banking official for an American firm in China. With the Chinese Revolution, the Petersons found themselves in the Philippines during the outbreak of World War II. It was there they were interned by the Japanese until the end of the war. As a consequence, their only daughter spent much of her childhood in confinement with other Americans and Western Europeans. The shared interests, perspectives, and relationships built out of that experience could never be replaced.

After release, the internees vowed to meet on a regular basis to renew friendships, reminisce, and socialize. Not surprisingly, the internees dispersed to many areas. An internee who was a newspaperman by profession printed a newsletter that carried information about the postwar lives of everyone involved. Quite by accident, several regions of the country had large concentrations of former internees. The San Francisco Bay Area was one such area. In his interview, Robert described the current status of that world.

> Quite a number of the people we got to know in the Far East have settled at Rossmoor (a San Francisco Bay Area retirement community). They are really the nucleus of a group of other internees that gets together about once or twice a year for sort-of a reunion . . . Sarah and I have sort-of skipped the last couple of years, but we do keep in touch with the people we still know. We are more inclined now to telephone than write. Of course, there have been a lot of casualties along the way. We've lost a lot of our friends and, as years go by, people get older and then drop out of the picture. For a long time, we had a newspaper that was put out by an old newspaperman. All the news he printed pertained to the people we met during the war. He's dead now and (laughter) I guess most of the people he wrote about then are dead now too. . . . People now just pass news around by word of mouth. Still, there is a reunion every year. In fact, this last year was the first time our daughter attended without us. You know, she really didn't know anyone who was there anymore. The younger people just don't seem to be holding this thing together the way we used to. . . .

It is important to analyze the observation that this world seems to be self-destructing. Unlike most social worlds, it is impossible to recruit new members. No outsider could share the internment experience. The shared perspectives, interests, and ideas linking these people were grounded in history. The relationships were located in a particular place and time. Perhaps the only additions to this world might be detached observers interested in historical, journalistic, or sociological approaches. Most of those who were adults during internment had died, or lost the interest, energy, or capacity to maintain the necessary linkages. Robert and Sarah Peterson had, along with their age peers, become valued resources within this world. With strong memories and images of the past, they were vital links in holding it together. Those who were children in the 1940s did not have the same closeness, commitment, and personal identification as their parents.

Integration into social worlds based on the people involved, rather than activities performed, is a risky proposition. When friends and acquaintances are actively involved, life in that world might be extremely rewarding. However, circumstances may arise that begin to destroy the very foundation of such a social world. Of course, worlds organized around specific people are few. Most are dominated by shared perspectives toward the creation of an object: art, music, dance, auto racing, sailing, and so on. Like most people, the aged tend to remain integrated into social worlds because of the activities they perform, rather than the people they meet.

Abandoning Old Worlds

While some social world involvements endure through the life cycle, others are abandoned. The abandonment or withdrawal out of a world that once provided social integration is the process most often associated with the aging experience. The aged are more likely than younger counterparts to abandon involvement due to relocation, disability, diminishing economic resources, or loss of personal allies. Retirement is another factor that seriously affects social world involvement of the aged. However, in and of itself, retirement does not force abandonment of all social world activities. More likely, different roles and activities, which continue to provide social integration, may be adopted.[3] For example, John Weston (Figure 2.1) was removed from his role as restaurant waiter through retirement. However, he then picked up related jobs that allowed him to maintain a modicum of social integration in the business world. While John probably was not as deeply integrated as he once was, meaningful activity continued. There are, of course, many worlds where rules regarding mandatory retirement do not seem to affect the activities of most aging people. The worlds of politics, government, art, and music are relevant examples. People may create art, serve in government, play music, and the like regardless of chronological age.

In this context, it is most important to focus on the process of abandoning social worlds. Emphasis, then, must be on the role of the process on aging lives, factors influencing the choices of older people, constraints on their activities, and personal meanings derived. For the moment, it is practical to set aside abandonment arising out of severe changes in family status, physical condition, economic resources, and residential location. The influence of these factors is the subject of detailed analysis in a later chapter. Instead, attention will be given to some instances of abandonment precipitated by relatively free choices on the part of aging people.

A theme which arose in nearly all interviews with older people was the notion that aging brings with it a kind of freedom not available to the young. Social constraints may be lessened, norms for proper behavior unclear, and obligations diminished. This is not to say that conceptions of age-appropriate behavior do not affect the everyday lives of the aged, but rather that ambiguity surrounding the role of the aged allows for variations in behavior (see Keith, 1982). For example, older people no longer tied down by rigid work routines had the freedom to sleep late, vacation at will, keep odd hours, take part-time jobs, and dress as they pleased.

Arising out of new-found freedoms, several aging people abandoned some social involvements to focus their energies on particular social worlds. A retired stock broker dropped out of several voluntary associations, neighborhood involvements, and business dealings to devote his time to social world activities like collecting, storing, preserving, and distributing foodstuffs for the gleaners. This world largely was comprised of retired people who kept half the foodstuffs collected for personal use and donated the rest to local charities. Several other people abandoned a number of social world involvements so they could focus their energy and resources on one activity. This was the case with an elderly bicyclist who became immersed in that world shortly after retirement. While his experiences will later be analyzed, it is enough to note here that his waking hours were consumed by the love of bicycling. He simply did not have enough time in the day, or intellectual energy, to pursue additional involvements with the vigor and intensity he felt they deserved. The world of bicycling, then, became the location of identity and the focus of energy because other involvements were abandoned. The two people here described may be exceptional cases. For example, they had the abilities and resources necessary to pursue their respective social worlds with the desired intensity. However, their experiences illustrate the extent to which personal meaning might be found in social worlds based in the present. They were not living in the past, but derived major portions of personal identity from current activities. Speculation about what the future held also were not of much concern. Current activities were simply too engaging to begin the search for acceptable substitutes.

EXAMPLE: ERMA MARTIN

The experiences of Erma Martin illustrate quite another aspect of abandonment. At the age of 66, she had been widowed for eight years, and her social life was marked by movement and change. Her most stable source of integration was the family. A divorced daughter lived with her and shared expenses. Frequent visits to her son in San Francisco were also sources of attachment and involvement. The rest of her life revolved around the search for meaningful integration. For several years after her husband's death, she attended a number of area churches. Few left her with any feeling of belonging although, at the time of the interview, she felt that one local church might be a good place to settle. An informal bridge group had also become something into which Erma wanted to be integrated. A number of close friends and neighbors were involved, and it was at their urging that she participated. In contrast, activity in an informal bowling group had not worked out. She expressed disappointment that everyone "took the bowling so seriously." Emma was more interested in entertainment, meeting new people, and perhaps finding a mate.

The process of abandoning social worlds accurately describes much of Erma's social existence. Like several others interviewed, she had been an active ballroom dancer for a few years after the death of her husband. It is interesting to note the primary reason she gave for abandoning ballroom dancing. While she was constantly searching for interesting, available men, dancing was also of great personal interest. Therefore, unlike some other social involvements pursued and later dropped, the activities of this world actually interested her. She went dancing on an average of three times weekly during the peak of involvement. Ironically, it was the attention of a male partner that stimulated abandonment. Erma and the partner had become quite close and met at the ballroom before each dance. Their partnership had begun to seep into other corners of life. The male partner wanted Erma to accompany him to dinners, meetings, and parties in addition to ballroom dancing. Convinced that he was going to propose marriage, she abruptly stopped dancing rather than have to decline the offer in a face-to-face situation. After abandoning dancing, she did not answer her telephone for some time in the hope that he would become discouraged. In essence, it was not that Erma was adverse to new relationships with men. Meeting men was a hidden agenda under-

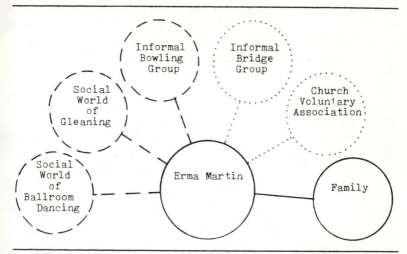

Figure 2.4: Profile of Erma Martin

lying much of her activity. Rather, it was the unwanted commitment of a certain man that instigated movement out of the ballroom dancing world. After a year or so, she sought to become reintegrated into the dancing circuit, but that also proved unrewarding.

The process of abandoning old worlds involves movement out of concerns which have come to be defined as meaningless. That is, the activities and concerns which integrate the person no longer fill the same role. In Erma's case, ballroom dancing no longer was enjoyable when she had to worry about interpersonal relationships. The fear of hurting her partner's feelings while rejecting his proposal overshadowed her love of dancing. In this example, the abandonment of a social world which had lost its meaning did not imply a move toward one more meaningful. In a sense, her experiences resemble those of people described in the previous section. They had become involved in social worlds because of the people involved, not the activities themselves. While this was not the nature of Erma's original involvement, it was the result of continued participation. On the other hand, the abandonment of some worlds in favor of bicycling and gleaning proved to be movements in the direction of greater meaning for the men earlier described. They were leaving places of diminishing interest for worlds of greater promise and prospects.

SEEKING NEW WORLDS

The process of seeking new worlds involves the attempt to meet new demands or situational contingencies. It is an effort toward which some of the aged devote cosiderable effort. For the most part, seeking is stimulated by crises of social involvement. Aging people may be retired, divorced, widowed, or disabled, and find some incentive for discovering new sources of social integration. For example, a chronic heart condition may force the abandonment of activity in some worlds. Dancing, bicycling, and hiking would be impossible. On the other hand, other social worlds demand less physical exertion of those involved. Stamp collecting, art appreciation, or photography may be pursued in ways that conform to the limitations of physical ability.

Of course, the aged do not all approach seeking in the same manner, nor with the same intensity. Many were not quite sure about what they were seeking, while others quickly assessed their needs and moved in appropriate directions. For Erma Martin and several other older women, the probabilities for meeting available men were weighed when considering one activity over others. More often than not, their decisions reflected compromises between interesting activities and proportions of unattached males likely to be present. Erma did not pursue involvement at the local senior center because, in her words, "the men there were either too old or already married." A relatively small number of aging people seemed to know exactly what they wanted in old age and set out to accomplish those goals.

However, there was a sizeable number of older people who had been seeking something of which they were not quite sure. Some recently retired, widowed, and relocated people found themselves gravitating toward various senior centers. They hoped to discover new activities and relationships in settings dominated by people of the same age, interests, and orientation. It was not so much that senior centers were the most attractive and interesting places for them, but they were the most obvious. Senior centers tended to be widely promoted, with newspapers publishing lists of current events. The aged visibly interacted in these settings.

Most interesting in this context, senior centers tended to be places where many social worlds intersected. That is, the organizers of these places had included a broad range of activities and involvements. Quilting, needlepoint, photography, watercolor, travel, carpentry, and genealogy were some activities found in many senior center rosters. These activities allowed the aged to taste and sample the activities of several different social worlds. Instruction in art, for example, seemed to allow the uninitiated to learn the basics of technique, style, perspective, and evaluation without risking humiliation among more experienced artists.

For the most part, the aged who tasted and sampled various worlds through activities sponsored by senior centers never left the protection of that setting to become more deeply immersed in those social worlds. That is, few people enrolled in photography, dance, or music lessons left the protection of the senior center to pursue those activities in the broader worlds inhabited by others performing similar functions. In fact, most who were active in senior centers expressed the desire to remain linked superficially into several social worlds. Senior center involvement, however, was given first priority. In this way, the older people found themselves segregated with others their own age. These people became peers who understood their lives, appreciated strengths, overlooked weaknesses, and allowed greater freedom of expression. These sentiments resemble those discovered by Arlie Hochschild (1978) in a working-class retirement community. The self-segregation of older people allowed a kind of freedom not found when younger people were present. The aged felt more free to reminisce, dance, and act foolish when they did not have to worry about being labeled senile or decrepit. With regard to involvement in senior centers, however, it is important to remember that only a small proportion of all older people engage in such activities (Atchley, 1980).

Finally, there is another aspect of seeking new worlds that must be mentioned. Many older people are relatively unsophisticated and naive in their knowledge about new involvements. Helena Lopata (1973) noted in her study of Chicago widows that these women were expected to become reintegrated after the crisis, but lacked the practical everyday knowledge by which to do so. For example, the use of organized social groups to develop new relationships and find integration depended on several things. First, knowledge of the groups and how to find them must exist. Second, ways of contacting representatives must be known. Third, the people involved must have some way of judging whether they will be compatible with the activities and participants they meet. Seeking includes an implicit ritual of involvement. This ritual was often unknown or unclear to older people who lacked a history of involvement of this type (Lopata, 1973: 246). Some widows fit this pattern since they depended upon the husband for knowledge, encouragement, and stimulation for social involvement. Without this stimulus, some recently widowed women felt as though they were floating free, unattached, and were not well integrated into society.

With regard to social worlds, the process of seeking is further complicated by heavy reliance upon networks of communication. Social worlds tend not to have storefronts or recruitment drives to draw in the uninitiated. As a result, many worlds lie concealed and undiscovered to those lacking the knowledge of how to tap into their linking devices. Therefore, the process of seeking new social worlds involves more elaborate knowledge than finding voluntary associations, formal organizations, interest groups, and territorial communities into which people are integrated.

Social worlds in aging lives may be rooted in the past, as well as the present. Involvements and activities in which the aged were no longer actively engaged have continued to be sources of integration through memories that provided linkages into social worlds. A fair proportion of time and energy in old age may be devoted to preserving memories of the past, as well as those of the present for future reference. These kinds of linkages, and their importance to the lives of older people, are crucial to a full understanding of social integration. Further, as shown in several of the case studies, activities of the present may revolve around maintaining certain involvements, abandoning others, and perhaps seeking new sources of integration. In essence, the role of social worlds in aging lives is constantly changing. Much depends upon individual perspectives toward the past, present, and future. With this in mind, the next chapter begins to analyze the evaluation and experiences of the aged in various social worlds.

NOTES

1. The experiences and lives of a number of individuals briefly will be used for illustrative purposes. At points throughout this chapter and others, then, the cir-

cumstances of nameless, faceless people will be used to supplement well-developed case histories and examples. In every case, these people later will be profiled in portions of the study where their situations are most appropriate.

2. While the gleaning world will be explained and analyzed later, a few words about it are in order. Gleaners are people who focus much of their time and energy toward the collection of unwanted foodstuffs. In Northern California, gleaning is wide-spread activity among older people distraught about the waste left by mechanical harvesting machinery. These people follow the machines through the fields picking up tomatoes, lettuce, apricots, peaches, grapes, and whatever else is left behind. This elaborate network of older people with trucks, storage space, canning equipment, and spare time was dispersed throughout California and the Sunbelt. Over the years, various gleaning groups had made contacts with other food producers who informed them if vast amounts of food was going to waste. For example, a Sacramento area ice cream maker contacted them and donated hundreds of half-gallons to them. The packaging machine apparently had folded the carton flaps in the wrong order, thereby rendering the ice cream unsaleable. Gleaning constituted a social world because many formally unconnected groups were united by the same perspectives and ideology. All kept half of the collected foodstuffs for personal use, and donated the remainder to local charities. In this way, the limitations of a fixed retirement income were transcended while, at the same time, assistance was given to those in greater need.

3. In a following chapter, the matter of retirement will be discussed in greater detail. It is a crisis in social integration that greatly affected the lives of many aged. It also was a problem handled in a wide variety of ways. These are topics to be explored later.

3

THE AGED IN SOCIAL WORLDS

By focusing on the aged in social worlds, it is possible to obtain a better understanding of an important aspect of social integration. Detailed knowledge of the everyday experiences of older people, the ways others evaluate their involvement, and relations between the young and old is the first step toward analyzing social world involvement from the perspective of the aged themselves. This chapter, then, begins a focus on the experiences, activities, and personal meanings of social world involvement among the aged that continues through the next four chapters.

To begin the analysis, the role of age in affecting the nature of social world integration is explored. Included in the discussion are matters related to the inclusion of the aged, effects of media use, role of weak authority, and effects of physical location on the everyday experiences of the aged in social worlds. The ways by which older participants were evaluated by others are illustrated through the use of empirical examples. The examples chronicle differences within social worlds classified according to the proportion of aged involved. That is, social worlds are described as youthful, age-mixed, and older according to the estimated proportion of older participants. Recognition of these tendencies is necessary for the focus on kinds of activities the aged perform that serve to integrate them into various social worlds and link them with others.

THE ROLE OF AGE

Throughout much of the sociological and gerontological literature, old age is considered an important variable that influences the ways older people are integrated into society. Advancing age is perceived to influence shifts from formal to informal participation in voluntary associations (Babchuk and Booth, 1969; Wilensky, 1961), withdrawal out of particular formal organizations (Atchley, 1976; Friedmann and Orbach, 1974), and a degree of social isolation in certain territorial communities (Bultena and Wood, 1969; Rosow, 1967). In addition, the onset of old age has been said to bring the elderly into contact with a variety of interest groups dealing with matters of old age (Pratt, 1976; Rose, 1965). For example, the Gray Panthers, American Association of Retired Persons, and similar groups orient their lobbying and publicity efforts toward the various causes of older people.

The influence of increasing age on involvement in social worlds is, perhaps, more subtle and less tangible than it is for many conventional forms of social organization. Heavy reliance on what have been termed conventional bases of social organization (e.g., formal membership, spatial contiguity, bureaucratic lines, and ascribed traits) implies that the age composition of the populations involved might be easily determined. Once the age of participants is determined, leaders in those forms of social organization could institute procedures to limit, or perhaps expand, the involvement of certain age categories. The late 1970s and early 1980s, for example, was a period where many social agencies sought to increase both numbers and proportions of the aged in certain housing units, fraternal orders, senior centers, lobbying groups, educational institutions, and the like. In these forms, increased numbers and proportions of the aged were rather easily assessed. Changes in formal membership could be measured, increases in bureaucratic roles occupied by the aged could be counted, and their presence in neighborhoods was observable.

On the other hand, the amorphousness, permeability, and spatial dispersion of social worlds makes an accurate enumeration of those involved a practical impossibility. Accurate statistical breakdowns on involvement by age cohort are unlikely. However, participants who were deeply integrated into various social worlds often had a sense for the numbers of older people involved. The proportion of aged participants in the bicycling world, for example, appeared to be quite small, while older people dominated worlds like those of ballroom and square dancing. Of course, the numbers and proportions of elderly involved in most social worlds would be located between these two extremes. In this context, the most important issues are related to the notion that social worlds are unable precisely to identify older participants, and that the influences of age are more subtle.

Inclusion of The Aged

The general statement that all social worlds include participants of many ages captures important characteristics of the phenomenon. It earlier was noted that social worlds encompass a very large population of people, united on the basis of shared interests and perspectives. It is inevitable, then, that all social worlds include at least a small proportion of older people. A focus on specific worlds would reveal them to be age-skewed in the sense that their central activities and roles are dominated by people of a certain age cohort. For example, the surfing and hippie worlds analyzed by John Irwin (1977) were dominated by very young adults. These were the people with interests in surfing and alternative lifestyles who, because they had vast amounts of free time, could formulate a philosophy to envelope those activities. The interviews with older people revealed that even the most youth-oriented world had some aging participants. The bicycling world was the best example of this fact. Several of the aged were visibly involved in this world, and managed to name many others who were also in their late 70s or 80s. Of course, it will later be explained that the dominance of young or old in a social world holds great implications for the everyday experiences of the aged.

On the other hand, there are retirement communities, senior centers, homes for the aged, voluntary associations, and lobbying groups exclusively for the elderly. What few younger people might exist within these forms must identify with the aged to survive. Social worlds are able to exert far less control over entry of age (or any other) groups into their domain. People of all ages may identify with the concerns of certain social worlds if they have access to any of their linking devices.

Effect of Media Use

Like all people in social worlds, the aged must rely upon various forms of media for vital linkages with others. Therefore, face-to-face interaction is not crucial for meaningful integration. It was apparent throughout the research that reliance on media also afforded older people opportunities to manage, conceal, or obscure knowledge of their age and abilities — often, in ways unavailable when they were acting in other social organizational forms. For example, the older stamp collectors described by Edwin Christ (1965) occasionally were integrated into networks of dealers and collectors who were largely unaware of the advanced ages of many participants. Much stamp collecting activity was accomplished through the mail or via telephone. In a sense, stamp collecting represented an activity that could easily be conducted despite the effects of advanced age. Chronological age simply did not seem to matter. Only when the older collectors appeared at auctions, conventions, and meetings where members of the stamp collecting world met face to face did their old age become apparent.

In this context, it is not important to note how many older people chose to obscure or conceal knowledge about their ages. Many were extremely proud of their advanced age and level of social involvement. Occasionally old age was flaunted when younger participants could not keep up, were not as successful, or lacked knowledge about social world processes. In this way, older participants demonstrated their competence, experience, and longevity to younger people. It was a way of proving social worth to those who might question it. Most important, at this point, is the fact that the potential for obscuring and concealing matters of age remained great. It was an option available to most older people in certain situations. Therefore, the option to conceal age selectively was invoked. For example, an older female artist submitted her paintings in an open competition. It was a rather large-scale affair, so the older artist knew that few would know her work. She had a friend deliver the painting to the place of competition lest the organizers learn the artist was older and partially disabled. Quite simply, the artist wanted her work to be evaluated for its merit, not because it represented the effort of a less than whole person.

Role of Weak Authority

The multiple and weak authority structures of social worlds makes a phenomenon like forced retirement highly unlikely. As acting bodies, social worlds simply do not have the strong centralized authority necessary to force actors completely out of their domain. Therefore, unlike formal organizations and some voluntary associations, people cannot be removed from this form because they have reached a certain age. Retirement may force aging people to adopt different roles, positions, and activities in social worlds, but complete removal is unlikely. For example, an art museum director may be removed from his job because of a city or private foundation policy on retirement. Despite this action, it is doubtful retirement would take with it the older person's love of art, artists, and the business. Retired museum directors may then have to resort to gallery employment, book writing, art collecting, or even creating art on their own to feel integrated in the art world. Throughout the interviews, examples of similar changes became apparent among people formerly employed in the business, stock market, and professional worlds.

Despite the lack of formal retirement policies, many worlds employ age categories to guide evaluation, structure competition, and encourage subworld formation. For example, chronological age has been a major line of cleavage within the bicycling world. The Veterans category ranges in age from 35 to 44; Masters are 45 through 54; and Grand Masters are 55 years of age and over. Most bicycling clubs have used these categories for the races, tours, and competitions they promote. However, in most instances the age divisions were rigidly enforced only during official or sanctioned events. Otherwise, they merely were intended to structure competition among age equals rather than force the withdrawal of older people from bicycling. The function of the age categories, according to several older people, was to stimulate increased involvement and interest among the aged. These divisions allowed for what the aged perceived as fair and good competition among peers. The demands of increasing age may be accompanied by subtle shifts in involvement rather than the abrupt pattern of integration/nonintegration associated with mandatory retirement in other forms of social organization.

Effect of Physical Location

Finally, residential location and the proportion of older people there is not an accurate indicator of involvement in social worlds. Throughout this study it has been argued that the shared interests and perspectives that unite people into social worlds transcend the confines of territory or place. However, physical location affects the kinds of activities people perform within social worlds and the degree to which they are integrated. For example, major figures of the art world must have regular face-to-face contact with artists, dealers, museum directors, benefactors, and the like to do business. Heavy concentrations of these people in a region facilitates the integration of those who love art. It is much easier to see the right exhibits, attend important functions, meet artists, and find colleagues in New York than it is in Kansas. Thus, while members of the art world exist in both places, their experiences and linkages differ.

Physical location, therefore, influences the collective or individual performance of tasks. Reliance on media for linkages implies that many activities and procedures in social worlds are performed apart from others. Robert and Sarah Peterson (Figure 2.3) maintained their ties to the worlds of World War II interness and art through letter writing, reading, television, and radio. These were activities individually accomplished. Only on rare occasions did the two of them meet with other members of these social worlds. The earlier described reunions represented some examples of infrequent face-to-face contact. Whatever collective activity existed in that world took place at the yearly reunions. It is also important to note that the infrequent meetings of the internees were influenced by the concentration of many people in one region. Perhaps if greater spatial dispersion of survivors had occurred, that social world would not have come together in the form it did. If routinized meetings had been impossible, the internees might not have felt the same needs and obligations to maintain the linkages over the years. Changes in physical location did not remove the Petersons from the worlds of art or internees. Relocation did, however, alter the modes of involvement and the frequency of personal interaction with others.

EVALUATING AGE IN SOCIAL WORLDS

All social worlds devise criteria by which the activities and contributions of participants are judged. The matters of determining the authenticity and legitimacy of actions, products, procedures, and judgments permeate much of that which social worlds do (Strauss, 1982). However, not all participants are judged and evaluated by the same standards. The evaluation of various products, actions, and performances rarely is entirely objective. Subjective assessments are made according to a broad range of social and personality traits. For example, the paintings or piano compositions of the mentally or physically disabled often are not evaluated by the same criteria as the contributions of "normals" might be in the worlds of art or music. In everyday life, a broad range of factors have been used to evaluate and judge the actions of individuals. Gender, race, sexual preference, and religion are common factors that encourage development and application of different standards of conduct.

In this context, the matter of age is first among the many possible factors affecting the evaluation of social world participants. Just as the contributions of children or youthful adults are evaluated by standards different from those applied to most others, so too with the aged. The matter of determining whether the standards applied to older people are more rigorous or lenient than others is highly situational. In some social worlds, old age may be a difference that is discrediting and shameful to those who hold the trait (Goffman, 1963). However, the social uncertainty and ambiguity surrounding old age makes it a weak stigma (Matthews, 1979: 57). The signs and cues which convey the presence of old age are contextual. That is, people may be defined as old in some situations because of a slight slowing of reflexes, or wrinkling of skin. These may be crucial standards for judging contributions. For example, the world of baseball has generated definitions of oldness which fit most players in their 30s. When timing and reflexes slow, some players have shifted to playing different positions, say from shortstop to first base, where their slowness of speed was not apparent. In this way, their careers have been extended. Also, the world of haute couture has defined models as old when they reach their mid-20s. The fierce competition and youth-oriented market made older models expendable. Changes in the age structure of society have, in some instances, extended the working lives of some models. As the baby boom generation ages, the nature of the buying public and marketing tactics has also changed.

As the preceding examples imply, vast differences exist among social worlds regarding the relevance of age. It also has been made apparent that a wide range of roles, activities, and options are available in social worlds that provide meaningful social integration. However, some people are more deeply integrated than others. The reasons for these differences are many, but generalizations may be made about the roles and positions of the aged in specific social worlds. The crucial activities of some worlds demand much energy, visual acuity, and stamina, while others do not. Therefore, based on interviews and observations, the experiences of older people in certain social worlds will by analyzed along three dimensions. First, the estimated proportion of older participants will be used to categorize some social worlds as youthful, age-mixed, or older. The tendency to concentrate on a portion of the entire life cycle says much about the lives of the aged. Second, within each category, probabilities for the aged to occupy roles of leadership and admiration will be weighed. This emphasis reveals the status of older participants. Finally, the overall evaluation of the aged by their fellow social world participants is of concern. In these ways, empirically based generalizations will be made about the place of the aged in specific worlds.

Youthful Worlds

Among the many social worlds incorporating the aged that emerged in the interviews, only two could be categorized as youthful. The worlds of bicycling and auto racing were not entirely made up of youthful people. Participants of all ages seem to be involved, but the largest proportion of people in roles of leadership, importance, and high visibility were youthful. In essence, these were worlds dominated by younger people whose energy, reflexes, resources, and stamina were appropriate for the demands of crucial activities. While definitions of youth are contextual, general use of the term in these worlds implied the dominance of young adults. Those of middle age might also have been considered youthful if they proved themselves through extraordinary capabilities, interests, or personal drive.

The youthful worlds of automobile racing and bicycling included older participants. For the most part, however, the aged were involved through relatively passive roles and activities. The older couple integrated into the world of auto racing was linked as spectators. At the ages of 65 and 63, they routinely attended Northern California stock car races. While this couple had been spectators for many years, the only change in their involvement as they reached old age was a slight decrease in the number of events attended. For the older husband, auto racing was extremely satisfying as he watched the "fruits of great mechanical ability." His long-time experience as a mechanic had served as the basis for his intense interest.

Largely because of their relatively passive involvement, the status and evaluation of their participation had remained constant over the years. They represented what gerontologists term the young-old. They were not so old that even active spectatorship aroused the interest of those around them. If they had been twenty years older even that activity might have seemed noteworthy. Similarly, if one of them had once been a stock car driver whose age had forced him out of competition, then their role as active spectators might have been evaluated as tragic, sad, or even pathetic. Drivers in the various subworlds of auto racing have been defined as old during their 30s and 40s. The physical endurance, perception, and reaction time required of people in such roles contributes to the definition of oldness arising in what ordinarily would be middle age. It is also interesting to note that many drivers reaching such ages have drawn upon the expertise and experience gained over the years to combat or compensate for declines in actual physical abilities.

It is also interesting to note that the role of spectator was institutionalized in the auto racing world. Few events have occurred outside the knowledge of spectators. Gate receipts, newspaper coverage, and television broadcasts have been crucial to the development and expansion of this social world. Such has not been the case in the world of bicycling. Bicycling events routinely have occurred outside the knowledge of potential spectators. Tours of several hundred or thousands of miles on open roads tend not to be conducive to the gazes of onlookers. The few spectators generally seen at such events probably have been close friends, spouses, or associates of participants. In terms of proportions, it seems that the bicycling world has included more people in relatively active roles and fewer passive ones.

For this reason, it is profitable to focus on the experiences of an older couple in the bicycling world. Their integration is noteworthy because of the very small proportion of older people involved in similar pursuits. Consequently, the evaluation of their activities by those within the bicycling world and the public at large was quite positive.

EXAMPLE:
FRED AND ALICE ROMANO IN
THE BICYCLING WORLD

At the age of 78, Fred Romano was a retired California Department of Transportation supervisor. Prior to his retirement, bicycling was an activity that had been dormant since his high school days. However, while repairing a highway in the Sierra Nevadas, Fred and his crew happened across a college professor from San Mateo on the first leg of a solo cross-country tour. In a long conversation, Fred learned from the bicyclist what the best new equipment was, what one needed to start bicycling, and decided to renew the activity as soon as he retired. At the age of 65, then, Fred took up bicycling and never looked back. He began a rigorous training schedule, joined local clubs, and began to get his feet wet in competitions. When he began competing, Fred said he was unsure about how he would be received. In his words, "I did not know what people would think about that strange man out there with younger fellas." Therefore, he adopted a nickname and had it emblazoned on his racing jersey. The nickname was something his grandchildren had applied to him and Fred thought it fit. Foxy Grandpa, as he came to be known, often found himself far behind the pack of other bicyclists, who ranged between the ages of 20 and 45. The nickname was intended to amuse onlookers as he wheeled by, chasing the main pack of riders. As he noted, "It gave me an excuse for coming in last. I guess it gave them something to laugh at, rather than at me personally."

Throughout Fred's career in the bicycling world, his wife Alice served as his staunchest ally. While not herself a bicyclist, she provided encouragement, served as his trainer, and attended nearly every event — whether or not Fred was competing. To a large degree, competitive bicycling is a sport dominated by men. Therefore, Alice found herself in the company of many younger wives and friends of other bicyclists. On long tours, Alice frequently accompanied the other women in their autos as they trailed the bicyclists carrying food, water, and spare parts.

In different ways, bicycling had consumed the lives of Fred and Alice. In terms of time spent, Fred's life was consumed by training, planning, traveling, and competing in bicycling events. Alice, on the other hand, had somewhat more free time on her hands. Therefore, while Fred had little time for friends or associations outside of bicycling, Alice felt the need to find sociability among other women. She was part of a small, informal group with which she attended movies, plays, and other events around town. Jointly, their children and grandchildren seemed to be the only other major source of integration. Their oldest son, at the age of 55, also was an avid bicyclist who competed in many of the same events as Fred. In fact, according to Alice, their son had only become interested in bicycling after Fred had renewed his long-dormant interest in it.

It is important to analyze closely the place of the Romanos in a world so clearly dominated by the young. During a criterium sponsored by a Northern California bicycling club, it was interesting to note which of the competitors won the hearts of the crowd because they were logically too old to be holding their own with much younger bicyclists. The darling of the audience was a 35-year-old man who, for a time, threatened to place in the longest of the many short races held on that day. Even though he did not win the race, the cheers on his behalf were testimony to public evaluation of his contribution. It is this kind of response that made Fred Romano's involvement so extraordinary.

In 1980, Fred completed a solo journey of 3100 miles in just over 33 days. It was a cross-country tour that took him from Northern California to his fiftieth college reunion in Worcester, Massachusetts.

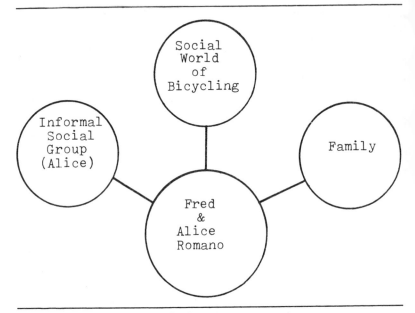

Figure 3.1: Profile of Fred and Alice Romano

Interestingly, it was the second time Fred had made exactly the same trip. Ten years earlier, he accomplished the same journey for the fortieth reunion. The 1980 tour, however, found Fred bettering his time of ten years earlier — and in the near-constant company of television crews and newspaper reporters. A major bicycling magazine, in fact, contracted with Fred to receive and publish his daily journal of experiences, trials, and tribulations along the way. Through this and other reporting, Fred found himself with many friends and admirers in many regions of the nation. Consequently, he had become a major figure in the bicycling world.

In a theoretical sense, Fred had become one of a small number of central figures in a social world who embody and personify nearly everything for which that world stands. He was an *exemplar* of the bicycling world who served as a model, idol, or archetype for the more ordinary of those involved. It became clear to many bicyclists that Fred approached bicycling with the fervor and dedication that aficionados seemed to believe demonstrated the way bicycles were meant to be ridden. In other words, he exemplified the true spirit of bicycling. For example, at the age of 77, Fred found himself recuperating from a broken leg received when he was struck by an automobile during a bicycling time trial. Crucial to his exemplar status was the fact that the injury was received during bicycling, rather than from a fall down some stairs or from some other everyday event. During recuperation, Alice noted that Fred thought only about returning to competition. He apparently felt he had to prove to others that his status in that world was not misplaced or unwarranted. His status, then, was achieved through the combination of age and determination.

The status of the Romanos in this social world was achieved and maintained through constant effort and dedication. Clearly, Fred and Alice had to devote more time and energy to maintaining positions of centrality in the bicycling world than would those of younger ages. However, there is another side to this point. It is also probable that the Romanos never would have achieved prominence had they not been older, more committed, and very dedicated to bicycling. Fred had not achieved the widespread notoriety and recognition at the age of 68 that he later had at 78. The fact that his performances seemed to improve rather than deteriorate with age was only icing on the cake. In fact, on the return trip from his Worcester, Massachusetts tour in 1980, Fred was asked to stop at a Washington University clinic in St. Louis for further study of his heart and muscle development. Even a relatively unpublicized event like this contributed to Fred's reputation. He later was the subject of a profile in a popular magazine related to the preservation of health and prevention of disease. It should also be noted that Fred did not shun publicity and, in fact, actively sought it. He was the one who informed area newspapers of his cross-country travel plans and, eventually, the final completion of the journey. His notoriety and recognition, then, had a strong element of self-promotion, as well as action which backed up his claims.

The preceding examples have illustrated a major problem found among older people in youthful worlds. When they were integrated through passive roles like those of spectator, viewer, and reader, they remained marginal. Involvement was not defined as distinctive, remarkable, or even noteworthy. Instead, the older people seemed to make up a proportion of other faceless, nameless participants. On the other hand, the adoption of an active role in a youthful world often brought instant notoriety. The widespread cultural belief that older people are tired, slow, and worn-out has encouraged people to notice those who have not fit the stereotype. While many of the aged in everyday life probably do not fit the popular conception, it is those who cavort among the young who seem most obvious.

Age-Mixed Worlds

Most social worlds which arose in the interviews with older people could be categorized as age-mixed. This means that younger, middle-aged, and older people alike were integrated and occupied positions of centrality and importance in these worlds. This is not to say that all age groups were equally mixed and distributed throughout various worlds. Rather, subworlds oriented toward one age group or the other have provided havens within the much larger, heterogeneous worlds.

In illustration of this point, it must be noted that the art world has included participants of all ages. Art museums, galleries, and art associations frequently have sponsored workshops and lectures designed to draw various age groups into that world. Particular attention has been directed toward the old and very young. Museums have had special admission prices for each of these age groups and have developed distinct tours. In many instances the events and activities designed by organizers of the art world to draw older people in have been located in senior centers, retirement organizations, or nursing homes. The general belief seems to have been that the acts of painting, sculpting, or photographing are means of self-expression for which many people have time only when they have reached old age. In his study of aging and the artistic career, the sociologist Hershel Hearn (1972: 361) noted,

> One of the reasons for late-in-life involvement in art for many people may be that art as a primary means of self-expression may have been less acceptable socially when they were young. The older they are now, the more this may have been true. . . . Older artists agree that art will be their work until they die. To them increasing age means increasing maturity and skill, and is viewed as an ally rather than a spector of gloom.

In essence, serious entry into the art world probably was not considered by some people before they reached old age because more pressing matters commanded their attention. There were bills to pay, children to get through school, jobs to go to, and careers to pursue. Hearn has also implied that social disapproval might have been felt if some older artists had forsaken the serious, instrumental pursuits of middle age for the expressive "frivolities" of art. It is interesting to note that the art world has included participants of all ages, yet has drawn in many people at the point of old age who previously had not expressed much interest in art.

For example, one of the older people interviewed found herself drawn in to the world of art for several reasons. While she did not consider herself old at 62, she had found herself with vast amounts of free time on her hands and she was partially disabled. She had suffered brain damage in an automobile accident while in her late 50s. Shortly thereafter, she was in the situation of being recently divorced, partially disabled, and alone. She seriously embarked upon an artistic career for the purposes of both personal expression and physical therapy. Through painting and sculpting, she sought to increase her manual dexterity and powers of concentration. Both had been diminished as a result of the accident. Her work had been shown in local galleries and the senior center. Advancing age, coupled with the disability, helped make her an object of some interest and admiration among the aged in her town. The knowledge others had concerning the obstacles she had overcome to create interesting, competent, and marketable art certainly did not impede evaluation of her involvement. At times, this artist knew that evaluations of her creations were charitable because of her plight, but she did not believe they arose out of pity.

An important characteristic of age-mixed worlds is the many nooks and crannies where older people may be involved but invisible. The previous example exemplifies this point. The older, disabled artist accomplished most of her artwork in solitude. She chose to paint, sculpt, and draw in the privacy of her apartment, and selectively entered public arenas to display her creations. Even less intense and more passive were the art world experiences of Robert and Sarah Peterson (Figure 2.3). Earlier, references were made to their integration into the Phoenix art world through various volunteer positions and offices. Through relocation to Northern California, they found themselves removed from personal contact with art lovers in age-mixed settings. Instead, they remained marginally integrated through the media. As Robert described it,

> I watch for what may be coming up on PBS. Their programs are really worthwhile. They often cover events at the White House, or have shows on various artists. In some cases anymore, it is just as satisfactory to read the reviews of some things than to actually attend the events. I don't have a very sustained attention span anymore. We also get a number of magazines which tell us about what is going on in the theatrical and art worlds. But, you know, that is about as much as Sarah and I have been involved in these activities.

While the Phoenix art world probably evaluated their involvement as reasonable when the Petersons were visibly involved, they became invisible with the move to Northern California. In a sense, they had moved in the direction of disengagement. They moved away from activities requiring the copresence of others, toward those that may be performed alone. In a personal sense, their involvement in the art world through the media was not known to other participants. The only recognition of involvement existed in the sense that other participants knew an audience was there, wrote articles with them in mind, filmed television specials, and sold them appropriate books.

The world of business was another prominent example that arose in the interviews. Several older men continued to identify with this age-mixed world dominated by those in middle age. The earlier described life of John Weston (Figure 2.1) illustrated the role of this social world in his later years. He had no dealings, investments, or contacts when interviewed that actively linked him into that world, but he relied on memories of deals and transactions in the past to sustain him. Older people who have been active in the business world long after the age of typical retirement may become exemplars. The late Harlen Sanders of Kentucky Fried Chicken fame founded his empire after the age of 65. To many, Colonel Sanders exemplified the ingenuity, tenacity, and good sense often associated with good business people. The fact that these traits became apparent in old age facilitated widespread recognition of his accomplishments. Also important in this example is the notion that older business people like

Sanders have not directed or oriented their accomplishments toward members of their own generation. Instead, the larger, age-mixed business world was the focus of their energies. It is a point of speculation that, perhaps, this focus accorded them greater recognition and respectability among younger people than efforts to develop products for the aged might. Success in the larger business world, with its highly competitive atmosphere, proved to those who matter that Colonel Sanders and his age peers still had the necessary drive to succeed.

Several other examples of age-mixed worlds arose in conversation. The worlds of music, dance, automobile collecting, and crafts are a few examples. At this point, it is useful to focus on the everyday experiences of one older couple in an age-mixed social world. In this example it is possible to understand the interpersonal evaluation of two older people who sought to become reintegrated into the world of square dancing. It was a world in which they once had been very active, lost their commitment for several reasons, and believed they could reactivate their interest as they approached old age.

EXAMPLE:
JACK AND GWEN HURLING IN
THE SQUARE DANCING WORLD

At the age of 62, Jack Hurling had been retired for two years from work at a Northern California cannery. He opted for early retirement after a long period of absence and recovery due to a massive coronary. At the time of the heart attack, Gwen took a leave of absence and later retired from her work as a receptionist to care for him. Both individually and as a couple, the Hurlings were integrated into a wide variety of social organizational forms. They lived near their son and his family. Family relationships always had been important and that continued to be so as they increased in age. They routinely had weekly dinners with their son, his wife, and grandchildren. They also lived in a mobile home park and enjoyed a certain degree of community there. The residents of that community regularly met to do repairs, formulate policy, and make decisions on shared concerns. Their joint foray into the world of automobile racing was chronicled

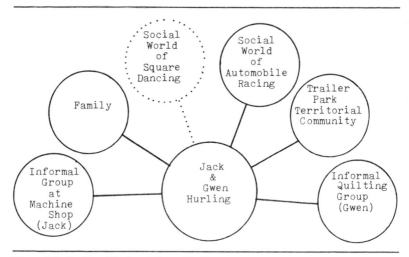

Figure 3.2: Profile of Jack and Gwen Hurling

earlier. They were spectators and had been attending stock car races for many years. Individually, each person had a stake in an informal group that provided another source of social integration. For Jack, it was a group that met irregularly at his machine shop to work on joint projects, share ideas, and socialize. Gwen had a similar arrangement with an informal quilting group that met about once a week.

The Hurlings were ardent square dancers during the early years of their marriage. Their involvement continued well into middle age as they regularly represented their Southern California club at regional conventions. As representatives of larger numbers of square dancers, it was implied that Jack and Gwen demonstrated the kind of commitment, technique, and ability others thought important. Through these activities, they made friends and met associates with whom they were in infrequent contact nearly twenty years after the square dancing meets.

When Jack began working at the Northern California cannery at the age of 49, the hard work and long hours forced them to withdraw from this social world. After a day of heavy lifting on the job, Jack simply did not have the energy or drive necessary for an evening of strenuous dancing. At that time, Gwen expressed a desire to continue dancing, but did not want to continue without Jack as a dancing partner. Therefore, she gave in to her husband's fatigue and partially withdrew from the square dancing world. However, several years after Jack's heart attack, the two of them began thinking about dancing. They initially did little to act upon these desires, but had expressed their wishes to some close friends who were also dancers. One evening when another couple failed to show up, their friends called asking them to come by and give it a try. Unsure of their abilities and Jack's condition, they went to the dance. They began very slowly and began to increase the pace of their dancing, as well as the duration. Over a long period of time, the Hurlings found themselves relatively well-integrated into this world once again. It was, however, their perception that they probably would never be as comfortable nor as competent in this world as they were during the years of middle age.

To understand the evaluation of Jack and Gwen's involvement in square dancing, it is necessary to step back and look at the state of that world. In the 1960s the square dancing world had the reputation of being an old person's concern. It was perceived to be old-fashioned, backward, and the domain of cowboys and Okies. While this image probably never was accurate, it did reflect the fact that the techniques and styles of square dancing were rooted in the past. This style of dancing was oriented toward simpler times. It had a strong, rural flavor with which some people in their later years could identify. At that time, then, the old made up a relatively high proportion of those involved in square dancing. In the minds of several older square dancers, however, the 1970s and 1980s saw a slight decline in proportions of aged involved. It apparently was not due to diminished interest of older people, but increased awareness and involvement by the young. In a sense, that period saw the square dancing world reach a stage of expansion and growth. Therefore, an image change had been in progress for several years before the Hurlings decided to reenter that world. Even though many older people were still involved, the influx of younger people had implications for the ways the aged would be evaluated.

The fact that Jack and Gwen were older than many fellow square dancers seemed to mark them as only mildly unusual. They were not that much older than many other participants. However, with Jack's return to square dancing, the combined effects of age and his heart condition made him an object of admiration. He was viewed by other dancers as good advertising for the perceived benefits of square dancing. They believed their activity to be both fun and strenuous. Therefore, the return of a recovering heart attack victim was seen as testimony to the benefits of the healthful, invigorating, and fun activity. Never mind that Jack occasionally slowed the pace of the entire group because of his diminished capacities, what mattered was involvement.

The preceding examples have illustrated the broad range of possibilities for the aged in social worlds that include many age groups. When subworlds or circles of the aged exist, it is probable that some older people would have roles of centrality, leadership, and importance. When pockets of the aged do not exist, it is perhaps more difficult for older people to continue or establish such positions. However, if they do, it is likely their involvement would be evaluated as positive, exemplary, or even remarkable. Such certainly was the case with Fred Romano in the bicycling world and, to a much lesser degree, Jack Hurling in the world of square dancing.

Older Worlds

Of the many worlds which arose in the interviews, only three could be classified as older. That is, there was a small group of worlds into which older people were integrated that focused upon interests or concerns of the aged. This is not to say that the middle aged or younger were not involved in these worlds, but rather that older people tended to hold positions of leadership and power. In essence, the aged were in control of the processes and activities of these worlds.

The first example of an older world is ballroom dancing. When compared with square dancing, this social world has been the exclusive domain of the middle aged and older. It was not infiltrated by the young during the 1960s and 1970s to the extent that the other dancing world had been. There was a small wave of nostalgia for the big band era, which brought with it some younger ballroom dancers, but the fashion seemed to fade away. Thus, involvement of the aged seemed to be the rule rather than the exception. It was as rare to find a ballroom dancer under 50 years of age as it was to find one over that age in the bicycling world. This characteristic has important implications for the evaluation of older people in ballroom dancing.

The music played at ballroom dances was largely that of the 1930s and 1940s. In addition, some dances were interspersed with the more classic waltzes, tangos, and foxtrots. Since this social world was formed and expanded during the post-Depression big band era, many of the older people involved had been active in the early years. That is, a good proportion of the aged who were involved had begun their ballroom dancing careers in late adolescence and early adulthood. For some, integration had remained relatively constant and stable over the years, while others had reentered upon the approach of old age.

In Northern California, the dances were held at fraternal lodges, hotel ballrooms, community centers, and retirement residences where large numbers of the aged were gathered. For a good portion of the year, ballroom dances were organized three or four times per week. For the most part, they were put together and run by older people themselves. However, some middle-aged community officials or senior center staff members occasionally had participated in the planning, publicity, and supervision of dances.

The lives of Lucy Anderson (Figure 2.2) and Erma Martin (Figure 2.4) in the ballroom dancing world were described earlier. At this point, it is fruitful to contrast evaluations of their involvement by fellow dancers. In this way, a better understanding of the role of age in an older world might be achieved. It was acknowledged that Erma Martin, at the age of 85, had been an active dancer for well over forty years. She danced four to five nights per week and had been integrated into a variety of ballroom dancing circuits as she traveled about the country living with each of her many children. Even in a world populated by the aged, Lucy often found herself dancing with partners many years her junior. Despite being widowed for forty years, Lucy claimed she had not become involved in this social world because of the possibilities for meeting single, older men. Rather, she simply loved to dance. Perhaps because of her advanced age, Lucy had not been perceived by others as someone looking for sustained male companionship. Whether or not Lucy truly was interested in finding a mate, the fact that she had not been considered by others to be available or marketable discouraged any attempts she might have made. In this older world, then, she seemed to be considered by some to be too old to be interesting (see Matthews, 1979).

The experiences of Erma Martin in the same ballroom dancing circuit were quite different. Her problems with a partner who had marriage on his mind were described earlier. In this context, it is important to note that Erma was perceived to be highly desirable by several other dancers. They thought her to be pleasant, financially secure, interesting, and a good dancer. Perhaps important in this estimation was the matter of age. Erma, at the age of 66, was relatively young in this world populated by the aged. Consequently, she had little trouble finding suitable male partners when she so desired. Most of the unattached men involved were older than Erma. Consequently, they did not have to deal with conflict arising out of the cultural expectation that males should be the older half of a couple.

In youthful and even age-mixed worlds, the assumption often is that old people are all alike. When the aged are a minority, other participants may act on the basis of stereotypes, thereby assuming that each and every older person is less capable or interesting than the rest. In worlds like ballroom dancing or World War II internees dominated by the old, these assumptions simply have not applied. In fact, relatively fine discriminations regarding age have been made. People in their 60s and 70s have been considered quite young in these worlds, while those in their late 70s and up truly were old. The following example of several lives in the gleaning world highlights some of the conditions under which discriminations based on age in older worlds have been made. The illustration includes those who might be termed the young-old as well as the old-old.

EXAMPLE:
HENRY FARLEY AND THE HARDINGS IN
THE GLEANING WORLD

Like the previously mentioned concerns, the world of gleaning was a concern dominated by the aged. This social world evolved out of the activities of Henry Farley, which began in 1976. A retired stockbroker, Henry had been involved in matters related to the aged and community activities since he was in his early 60s. In 1976, at the age of 75, Henry learned of a semi-truck trailer loaded with fresh bread that had overturned on the freeway near Bakersfield. The baking company was looking for a group willing to pick up the cartons, transport them, and deliver them to charity. Somehow, Henry learned of the problem and commandeered several large trucks from friends in Northern California. He completed the mission, and this was the beginning of an elaborate network that later would be constructed around the discovery, transportation, and delivery of previously wasted foodstuffs. Henry had long been concerned with the large-scale waste of produce in the Sacramento Valley in California. Mechanized harvesters had been developed to retrieve only the most desirable products, thereby leaving huge amounts of smaller, bruised, or buried food behind.

Utilizing organizational abilities formed in the business world, Henry identified the aged as the population best suited for the work and benefits of gleaning. In his words,

> Old people seemed to have the most free time on their hands. You know, with this kind of work, you have to be able to pick up at a moment's notice. Peaches on the tree or tomatoes in the field can't wait until the weekend, or until you have a little free time. With inflation and the limited income of the retired, gleaning is also a good way of getting some very good things for next to nothing. Some of the women involved have put out recipes and canning ideas for all the stuff we have gotten over the years.

The group began with only 37 participants in 1976. Through his personal recruitment, it mushroomed to several hundred in a few years. Henry Farley attended meetings of Kiwanis Clubs, Chambers of Commerce, Rotary Clubs, and senior centers trying to recruit people into gleaning. He and a core of original members did not restrict the participation of any age group. However, the requirements of need and free time resulted in an overwhelming majority of older participants. From the beginning, Henry's conception of the gleaning world was that the aged would keep one-half of the foodstuffs for themselves and donate the remainder to charities. In a period of less than five years, the gleaning idea had spread from the Sacramento Valley to the Salinas Valley, Southern California, Texas, Florida, and other portions of the Sunbelt.

Henry Farley was from the beginning a central figure in this social world. He originated the idea of an activity system devoted to gleaning, and created the vital linkages that maintained the network of older people, growers, distributors, and charities revolving around the concept. In a theoretical sense, Henry was an *organizational leader* whose activities included every subcategory of the term. First, he was the *founding parent;* his ideas and activities led to initial formation of the social world. Second, he was its *intellectual leader,* and developed the rationale, philosophy, and guidelines that created the system of shared perspectives and ideas linking older people together in ways transcending geographical space. Finally, he was the *social organizational leader;* his activities kept the gleaning world together. The recruitment of new participants, the training of new leaders, and the organization of materials were matters that fell on him in this capacity.

Because of the degree to which gleaning was embedded in his life, Henry Farley had little time for other activities. In effect, gleaning consumed his life. The only other form of social organization into which he was integrated was his family. Still, he offered little detail about his family life. Gleaning seemed to be too important. While he maintained memberships in voluntary associations like the Chamber of Commerce, Kiwanis, or Rotary Club, these involvements were kept only for their value in spreading the word about gleaning.

Henry Farley's original concept was that all people in need could participate in gleaning, even though the design was to create meaningful involvements for the aged. Consequently, because several universities and colleges are located in the Northern California area in which gleaning began, it was probably inevitable that some students would become involved. The gleaners were especially receptive to students with families who, without inexpensive produce, probably would not have survived on their limited incomes. However, this point led to a bitter feud in 1978.

At that point in time, Henry had become the symbolic leader of many gleaning chapters located across California. All but the chapter nearest Henry had placed strict limitations on the age of those who could participate. That is, all but one group had limited involvement to the elderly. The ensuing feud was focused on this issue. Eventually, largely because of the sheer numbers of the aged involved in the gleaning groups, Henry Farley was ousted as leader and organizer for

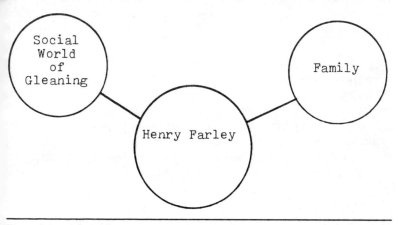

Figure 3.3: Profile of Henry Farley

all the groups. All groups but one did not see the value of including participants of all ages. Most gleaners did not live in areas where they saw large numbers of needy college students. Consequently, they believed that the activity was best left for members of the older generation. In their minds, the elderly clearly were the most deserving group, and were the ones who had devoted vast amounts of time, energy, and resources into developing the social world. The end result was that the once-cohesive world of gleaning split into two competing subworlds. The Senior Gleaners ousted Henry Farley from his symbolic roost. They became the largest gleaning group and took with them a good portion of the resources, contacts, and participants. The Statewide Gleaners were those who remained loyal to Henry and his plan to integrate age groups into that social world.

Thelma and Thomas Harding were two participants remaining loyal to Farley and the Statewide Gleaners. They had become familiar with this social world through one of Farley's speeches at a local senior center. At the time they said they were struck by the charitable nature of the activity, as well as the prospect of extending their limited retirement incomes. Both had been thrifty all their lives, but found that their pensions left them with little extra money at the end of each month. Over time the Hardings became central figures in the relatively small subworld of the Statewide Gleaners. Their front porch became the distribution point for much of the foodstuffs gathered during the week. Further, Thelma had become head of the "telephone tree" by which other participants were informed of a planned pickup and distribution. Henry Farley would call Thelma to tell her of an important contact made, the place for pickup, and time of arrival. She then telephoned a predetermined list of other women who, in turn, would call another list of participants. In this way, a relatively large number of older people were mobilized in a very short period of time. Simultaneously, Thomas probably would have left in his pickup truck to meet other gleaners at the site. They would then pick the cherries, gather the squash, or harvest the grapes and deliver them to the Hardings's front porch.

In a theoretical sense, the Hardings' home served as an *organizing center* for the gleaning subworld. It was the site of much activity coordination and organization. Much of the information necessary for participation was disseminated through the Hardings and their contacts. Their home was also a *meeting place* where foodstuffs were distributed, potluck dinners were held, and the canning of fruits took place. Of course, there were other sites serving similar functions. For example, the newsletter publicized activities of participants, news of recent gleaning triumphs, and recipes for preparing whatever had been collected over the past week was published out of another member's home.[2]

However, unlike Henry Farley, the Hardings had not allowed gleaning to consume their entire lives. They were long-time residents of the same community and, consequently, had many sources of social integration. Like many of those interviewed, they had a long and stable involvement with their family. They lived near their children and regularly interacted with them. The larger community had also been a focus of much activity for them over the years. They regularly participated in various charitable drives and fundraisers, which further conveyed their community spirit. Individually, Thelma was the organizer of an informal arts and crafts group that met at her home. A few of those involved also were active in the gleaning group. Thomas, at the time of the interview, had just received an award from the Masons for forty years of continued service. The longevity of his social involvement was a source of great pride. Finally, the local

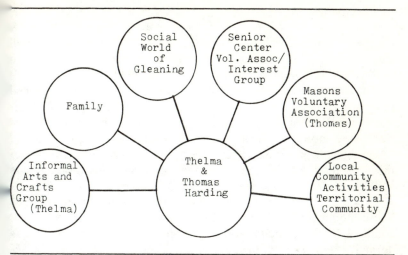

Figure 3.4: Profile of Thelma and Thomas Harding

senior center had been a focus of some activity for them over the previous five years. As the profile below implies, they did not have vast amounts of free time, but liked to drop in and see old friends on occasion.

In a comparative sense, the stability of social involvements for Thelma and Thomas Harding was remarkable. They had managed to construct a diverse but stable postretirement life at the ages of 65 and 67 respectively. Also surprising is the degree to which they were deeply integrated into several social organizational forms despite the diverse demands on their time, energy, and resources. Their integration into the gleaning world is the best example. This social world involvement was not oriented toward the fulfillment of creative or expressive needs. Rather, it was instrumental and allowed them to extend their fixed retirement income. In many ways, they treated gleaning as they once did their employment. When there was gleaning work to be done, they simply set aside other less pragmatic concerns. Therefore, involvements such as the senior center or the informal arts and crafts group were used to fill the spare time that gleaning and family concerns had not filled. It was the precedence the Hardings gave to the gleaning world that contributed to a high evaluation of their activities. Perhaps only Henry Farley and a few others surpassed them in terms of commitment, energy, and availability. A number of other older people interviewed who had been involved in gleaning seemed considerably less willing to drop everything when notification of a food pickup came.

Importantly, the nature of older worlds demands that the aged occupy positions of leadership, as well as the rank and file. Consequently, the evaluation of older participants within specific worlds was based more on the qualities and performances of the people, rather than the presumed value of the aged in general. Participation of the aged tended not to be evaluated as extraordinary, or perhaps irritating. Instead, it was expected and normalized within the context. Clearly, exceptional individuals like Henry Farley existed in other worlds dominated by the old. When knowledge of their activities was confined to other social world participants, they were viewed as normal, everyday activities. However, when news of extremely active, knowledgeable, and physically fit older people has reached many outside the context of the social world in which the qualities were displayed, the aged have been evaluated as extraordinary individuals. They were viewed as examples of those few aging individuals for whom the stereotypes do not apply.

The contexts within which older people display their talents, abilities, and interests have much to do with the evaluation of them by others. This chapter has explored some differences in evaluations located in youthful, age-mixed, and older worlds. With these observations and examples in mind, it is important to confront the ways by which the aged become integrated into social worlds. That is, there is a broad range of activities by which older people have established and maintained linkages into various worlds. The nature of the activity performed holds tremendous implications for the degree to which older people are integrated, their experiences with others, and the effects of various age-related changes in their lives.

NOTES

1. As in Orrin Klapp's (1962) discussion of "heroes, villains and fools," it is likely social worlds also generate central figures who are contemptible or ineffectual.

Similarly, a number of social world processes or activities would be oriented toward these figures. In this discussion of *exemplars,* the focus has been on those central figures which Klapp would have termed "heroes." The generation of social world heroes is both a crucial and pervasive phenomenon. It is a process which holds great social organizational importance. The more ordinary among the people involved orient their activities toward the standard set by heroes. Similarly, villains and fools facilitate the definition of other boundaries. They help define the limits of negative behavior, poor performance, demeanor, and the like.

2. The notions of *organizing centers* and *meeting places* illustrates the importance of geographical space in social worlds. Even though the boundaries and influence of social worlds transcend territory, the activities and processes of social worlds must occur in time and space. That is, the processes of organizing and meeting other participants must occur, at least occasionally, in the copresence of other people. In this sense, social worlds also tend to devise *training centers* where novices go to learn the necessary skills for deeper integration or greater recognition in social worlds. Training centers in some social worlds may take the form of camps, seminars, schools, lectures, and workshops where vital skills are imparted. While not everyone involved in a social world must attend training at a training center, it often is a mark of upward mobility to do so. It is there that certain paths and strategies for advancement are imparted to people for whom they would otherwise have remained undiscovered. For example, workshops on automobile restoration have clued interested restorers and collectors to certain details that catch the eyes of judges (Dannefer, 1980). Also, Barbara Rosenblum's (1978) study of three subworlds in the world of photography has noted the importance of training centers in learning the fine points of advertising, fine arts, and news photography. Of course, other kinds of activities also occur in geographical spaces. These spaces may become focal points toward which much time and energy is directed, whether or not actual visitation occurs. These might be termed social world *meccas.* New York's Broadway is a mecca for the many thespians and aficionados of the theater who live in the region, as well as in the hinterland. Many never actually visit this theater district, nor directly benefit from its performances. Still, much attention may be focused on that space. Finally, social worlds also tend to conduct and create activities in spaces where participants meet one another face to face and engage in organizing, training, or standing in reverance of others' accomplishments. The different orientations are illustrated in the following list: (1) *conventions* are held where issues, ideas, and rules are debated and exchanged; (2) *auctions* are organized for the exchanging, bartering, and selling of certain types or classes of items; (3) *exhibits* are created where the products or creations important to a social world are displayed and evaluated; and (4) *meets* may be held where the various talents of participants are displayed, competitions are held, and evaluations are offered. The evaluations offered may either be from peers, or from an objective judging body.

4

AGE AND INTEGRATING ACTIVITIES

The corpus of knowledge, perspectives, practices, and activities that make up social worlds is structured very much like a whirlpool. That is, social worlds tend to have a central core wherein organizational leaders and other central figures are located. These are the people whose lives probably have been dedicated to the on-going functioning of that particular world. Movement outward from the core, then, implies somewhat less intensity of involvement and, for the most part, diminished personal meaning derived from involvement in that social world. Once again, like a whirlpool, the intensity of involvement probably decreases as people find themselves located at points away from the central core or hub of activities. The point at which the knowledge, perspectives, practices, and activities of a particular social world no longer hold meaning for actors is, as it earlier was explained, considered the boundary of a social world. The imagery of integration, then, is that of a whirlpool that barely affects the lives of those on the periphery and increases in intensity as people move more deeply into its structure. With that movement it is likely the meaning of personal involvement and integration would increase.

The activities people perform in a social world say much about their location within this whirlpool. There are many ways by which people maintain linkages into particular worlds, but they are not equal in status or ability to deeply integrate them into the concerns of those worlds.

This chapter is concerned with the matter of age and its effect on the activities by which older people have been integrated into particular worlds. Even though it has been said that all social worlds include a proportion of older participants, important differences have been implied with regard to ways the major characters of this study were linked into youthful, age-mixed, and older worlds. The older people who were integrated into younger worlds tended to engage in activities that situated them near the periphery of social world involvement. Clearly, those who engaged in central activities were considered exceptional individuals. On the other hand, older worlds have demanded the performance of a broad range of activities by the aged. By focusing on the ways in which the aged have maintained integration in various social worlds, a generalized portrait of older people in this form of social organization may be developed. Eventually, in later chapters this portrait will be supplemented to include an analysis of the everyday experiences of older people — including the phenomenology of involvement. Also, movement of the aged through various activities will be given some attention as they change their degrees and modes of integration. At this point it is important to focus on the activities integrating older people at certain points within social worlds.

INTEGRATING ACTIVITIES

With the whirlpool imagery in mind, there is a set of eight *integrating activities* locating people at various points from the periphery of a social world to the core. In that order, the set consists of *consuming, collecting, creating, performing, marketing, organizing, representing,* and *evaluating.* Like all actors, the major characters of this study were tied to the concerns of particular social worlds through at least one of these activities. Of course, it was also true that many of them were engaged in more than one of the eight integrating activities. The activity locating the older people nearest the core of specific social worlds is most important to this discussion because it signifies the degree to which the structure had been penetrated by the aged. It will become apparent that the activities probably have not been equally distributed among the aged involved in specific social worlds.

Consuming

The inclusion of *consuming* as an integrating activity is intended to acknowledge and legitimize the importance of watching, viewing, reading, listening, and simply being an observor for integration into social worlds. While most of the pursuits included in the term are passive, they may supply people with a modicum of personal meaning. In essence, they are ways by which individuals are located within the boundaries of a social world, albeit near the periphery.

Individually, those who consume the materials, activities, and objects a social world creates are invisible to those who are more deeply integrated. This is not to say that central figures do not recognize consumers as vital components to the structure of a social world. Clearly, many products and performances have been created specifically for the purpose of consumption by others. However, consumers as a group are nameless, faceless entities who generally are recognized by those more deeply integrated as a mere category of marginal people. In a very real sense, those who engage only in consuming truly are leading invisible lives in social worlds.

Still, this activity has linked huge numbers of people into many different worlds. The case of Robert and Sarah Peterson (Figure 2.3) is the best example of older people who had continued somewhat marginal integration into a social world at an advanced age. They continued linkages into the art world via television, magazines, and journals. In a very real sense the act of consuming what the art world produced situated them near the periphery. This was because they previously had been more deeply integrated and, for a number of reasons, found themselves engaged in activities they considered to be of less importance than earlier ones. In their minds, consuming represented an outward move within that world. For Jack and Gwen Hurling (Figure 3.2), on the other hand, consuming what the auto racing world produced was a long-standing concern. As spectators they perceived themselves to be integrated into that social world to the same degree they always had. For still other aging people, consuming represented the first step toward greater integration. Several older people, who eventually were deeply involved in the worlds of art, photography, dance, and genealogy, began their careers by consuming the products others created. For them, this activity was the first step in the process of learning the rules, procedures, criteria, and rationales for that which others in the social world produced.

Those few older individuals who found great personal meaning by consuming tended to approach it with a high degree of fervor, intensity, and passion. If they were consuming works of art, as the Petersons and others did, they tended to become relatively selective in the kinds of art they wished to consume. In many ways the process of becoming an informed and intelligent consumer of the products of any given social world was the ingredient that made this integrating activity meaningful for the older people interviewed. Such was the process through which these consumers learned to distinguish between good and bad social world products. In essence, the role of active consumption sharpened the analytic and critical powers of the older people adopting that stance.

For many of the aged, consuming was an activity toward which they devoted increased proportions of time as interest waned, or physical abilities declined. For some, consuming once was one of many integrating activities supplying them with personal meaning and integration. Over time, it eventually constituted the only remaining link (see Gordon et al., 1976).

Collecting

A second integrating activity which has located people somewhat more deeply into the domain of social worlds is *collecting*. This is an activity implying greater knowledge of the products created by social worlds than mere consumption. To be a collector implies the conscious accumulation of certain objects and materials, but several orientations were formed toward this activity. Collecting may impulsively be pursued, or an arbitrary system of logic may be imposed that guides the selection of object and materials (see Dannefer, 1980). Impulsive collecting occasionally results in the large accumulation of seemingly unrelated items. These collections generally do not represent fine, knowledgeable, or discriminating choices on the part of the people involved. Instead, they consist of items vaguely having something to do with stamps, bicycles, coins, art, and so on. For example, one older artist began her career in the art world by collecting books, magazines, and art prints. Her tastes were best characterized as eclectic and exploratory. Eventually, after she had gained somewhat greater knowledge and exposure, she began to impose restrictions on further materials and objects to be collected. She narrowed her focus to books on the sculptor Henry Moore, Asian art, and painting techniques. In essence, once a large body of vaguely related items was compiled, a logical set of categories was devised that rendered some previous efforts sensible, and set the tone for later collecting.

A second orientation, selective collecting, is guided by a well-defined system of logic by which the value of objects for collecting is guided, defined, and evaluated. Such a system may be predetermined and generated within social worlds for those who would become collectors. The most valuable and, perhaps, meaningful coin collections are those conforming to logical sets developed by others. The condition of the coin, composition, mint location, date of issue, historical period, and uniqueness are but a few relevant factors legitimizing collections. Regardless of what is being collected, this orientation forces the person to study and learn the complex system lying within that world. In this way, people are drawn more deeply into the structures of social worlds than they once had been.

In his study of retired stamp collectors, Edwin Christ (1965) noted how stamp collecting was an activity carried over from preretirement years. It was an activity in which age presented no barrier to continuity. This observation probably holds true for all collecting and its value as an integrating activity. That is, the process of collecting objects produced by a social world did not seem to be affected seriously by matters associated with increasing age such as declining physical abilities, decreased mobility, and diminished income. Of course, these factors may affect the kind and quality of individual's collections. For example, older collectors may need rare stamps, coins, works of art, or whatever to fill in gaps found in their collections. However, the activity itself is one allowing a great deal of flexibility in dealing with such matters on an individual basis.

While collecting was not an integrating activity widely pursued by most of the older people interviewed, it represents a means toward which they might move as increasing age makes other activities problematic. For example, while Fred and Alice Romano (Figure 3.1) had spent many hours collecting, organizing, and classifying materials about their involvement in bicycling, it was not their majour source of integration. However, had something happened to Fred making bicycling impossible, it is likely more time would have been devoted to their collection of bicycling memorabilia. When collecting was a major source of integration among those interviewed, it generally represented a way station on the way out of or into a social world.

However, collecting as the sole source of integration does not allow for very deep immersion or widespread recognition within a social world. It is important to note several implications of this notion for the lives of older people. First, if collecting were an activity remaining constant over the life span, it is likely the older person was never a central figure in that world. The activity probably involved so many other people that it was rare for any one collector to achieve prominence. Of course, exceptional collectors have rare collections that achieve widespread recognition and acclaim. Such was the case with Bill Harrah's automobile collection in Reno, Nevada. Second, if collecting had become an integrating activity assumed because other integrating activities had become too difficult or dangerous, it was likely the older person lost a modicum of status within that social world. Such would certainly have been the case if Fred Romano had stopped racing and touring to devote his time to collecting. In most instances, the backward movement toward collecting marked the beginning of continued disengagement.

Creating

A third emphasis situating people even more deeply in social worlds is *creating* that which the specific worlds produce. Use of the term is restricted here to the creation of concrete, tangible objects like paintings, writings, compositions, photographs, musical instruments, dance routines, automobiles, and bicycles for their respective social worlds. These creators are actors around whom many social world activities swirl. In fact, some serving in the formation of social world development may be conceived of as founding parents, organizational leaders, opinion leaders, and exemplars. For this to occur, the creator must also possess organizational interests and capabilities, or be surrounded by interested colleagues who can provide these talents. A photographer like Alfred Stieglitz managed to turn his interest in creating into a widespread, publicly recognized pursuit only by devoting considerable time and energy to organizational matters.

Of the older people interviewed, only Henry Farley (Figure 3.3) approached this level of dedication by coupling creating and organizing. In effect, he created and formalized the activity of gleaning by providing the structure and rationale for others to follow. Just as photographs existed before Stieglitz, so too with scrounging wasted foodstuffs before Henry Farley. Yet, through the activities of each, the creation of photographs and the canning and distribution of wasted foodstuffs was legitimized for particular populations. Once again, it is worth noting that Henry Farley's activities were focused on a social world inhabited by older people wherein he could obtain a position of leadership and hope to alleviate the inadequacies of old age pensions.

The other older people who had engaged in creating tended to bring those activities with them into old age. Those who painted, quilted, knitted, worked with wood, and the like had learned those skills during their younger years. This same phenomenon has been documented by other gerontologists interested in creativity during old age (Atchley, 1980; Hearn, 1972; Keith, 1982). For the elderly to achieve widespread recognition for creative activities engaged in during old age, self-confidence, professional contacts, economic resources, and in-depth social world knowledge would be required. As earlier noted, this kind of commitment and interest is something many older people did not possess.

Most important, however, the activity of creating began to locate and situate the older people more deeply into the structures of various social worlds than had consuming and collecting. Consequently, those people who first engaged in creating, while moving away from consuming or collecting, were taking steps in the direction of greater integration. In terms of increased knowledge and familiarity with social world processes, the step toward creating was crucial.

Performing

Much like people who create what social worlds produce, those who *perform* various activities tended to be more deeply situated in social worlds than either consumers or collectors. In essence, all social worlds include activities, functions, skills, and tasks that must be executed by individual people. Through these activities, those who are involved demonstrate to others their abilities and knowledge of things their social worlds value. In fact, many social worlds are known and characterized by the primary activities their participants perform. Such is the case with bowling, bicycling, gleaning, and dance.

For the most part, performing requires some kind of public presentation or display. That is, the performance of many activities requires the presence of audiences, consumers, viewers, and fellow performers. Even if the performance of various activities is accomplished outside the gaze of others, a certain degree of social integration exists simply because the person must have a rudimentary understanding of the techniques and styles required. However, those who perform in the copresence of other social world participants probably are more deeply integrated than those who do not. Acknowledgment and affirmation by other participants is a stimulus toward greater involvement. For example, those who bowl alone may identify with the larger bowling world, but it is unlikely they would be as knowledgeable as those who have bowled in leagues, tournaments, and with friends.

Through the constant comparison of experiences and perspectives with others, people tend to acquire a greater breadth of perspective toward social world events, activities, and processes than they would if they simply had relied on the media for vital linkages (see Warshay, 1962). The experiences of Arnold and Jean Goodrich (Figure 1.2) as well as Fred and Alice Romano (3.1) in the worlds of bowling and bicycling illustrate this point. By performing these activities, they found themselves deeply immersed with others who shared similar interests. In both instances they utilized the in-depth knowledge acquired to meet new friends during their travels.

For the most part, older performers tended to engage in such acts in worlds where the physical demands were not excessive. Most bowlers, golfers, musicians, and dancers had managed to adapt the performance of those activities to meet their changing needs and capabilities. Even Fred Romano was able to alter his training program and competition schedule to compensate for the broken leg he received in an automobile accident. The elderly ballroom dancers, however, found it easier to alter their performances than did some square dancers. Ballroom dancing was a couple-based activity, while square dancing required the coordination of a much larger group. When the performance of a square dancer was altered or impaired, the continuity of the entire group was slightly disrupted.

Marketing

The act of selling or purchasing that which other people in a social world create is another way by which integration is achieved. Unlike consumers, collectors, creators, and performers in a social world, those who engage in *marketing* may have had an affiliation with a formal organization. For example, those who deal in art objects, stocks, or antiques often have home bases at museums, galleries, or institutions. Through such affiliations, many engaged in marketing have created more elaborate networks of clients, sellers, and buyers than those who lacked such bases. Formal organizations within various worlds have the capital, resources, procedures, and past histories that facilitate contacts for those engaged in marketing. Therefore, the shift to marketing begins to immerse people deeply into the activities of specific social worlds. The act of marketing that which others produce necessitates substantial knowledge of the standards by which other participants evaluate the authenticity, legitimacy, and value of certain objects or products. Such knowledge can only be developed through experience and exposure to the processes and activities of various social worlds.

With this in mind, it was apparent that formal retirement had removed many older people from this integrating activity as old age approached. Clearly, retirement from organizations which had provided the institutional bases for marketing activities removed several of the older people interviewed from vital networks of contacts. The retirement of John Weston (Figure 2.1) from the restaurant business was the final stage in his long and gradual move toward the periphery of the business world. With the loss of the base through which John Weston could engage in marketing, the only linkage remaining was continued involvement through the media. Without the interest or resources to begin a new business interest in old age, the media became his only source of integration. On the other hand, the stockbroker Henry Farley (Figure 3.3) found himself without an institutional base from which to pursue his interests and talents in marketing after retirement from the brokerage firm. He then directed his attention to the matter of gleaning wherein his marketing talents could be redirected and applied. In this instance, knowledge and experience derived out of involvement in one social world facilitated rapid integration into another.

Marketing was also an activity in which some older individuals engaged without the benefit of institutional bases. In a sense, they were solo marketers who relied upon their own knowledge and resources for this activity. The retired stamp collectors described by Edwin Christ (1965) and the old-car collectors portrayed by Dale Dannefer (1980) represent good examples of this approach. In both instances marketing was a logical and natural extension of collecting. It consisted of buying and selling the things they had been collecting. Through collecting, they learned the values and criteria for evaluating stamps and automobiles. The activities of buying and selling were natural for them as they sought to give their collections greater integrity. They sold the stamps and automobiles that did not fit in with their planned collections. In essence, through marketing they managed to increase the value of their own collections. For these reasons, older people involved in marketing had demonstrated their commitment through efforts requiring long hours of study to keep up with changing trends.

Organizing

All social worlds include a small number of people who are *organizing* important events, activities, and processes for others. Very much like marketing, this integrating activity requires intimate knowledge of social world procedures and components. In many ways organizing more deeply integrates people into social worlds than any of the previously described activities. The matter or organizing the activities of other participants demands an awareness of the location, characteristics, and abilities of individual people. It also requires knowledge of the linking devices employed and the ways they might selectively be utilized to disseminate information. For example, organizers of the ballroom dancing world had to know which newsletters, radio stations, senior centers, and civic organizations to contact regarding publicity for various dances. In essence, these people had to know where the boundaries of their social world were, and how they might be manipulated. They did not want to publicize a dance designed to attract older people in a media that would be received mostly by middle-aged to younger couples. The dances oriented toward the elderly simply demanded use of different linking devices. The organizational leaders, founding parents, and opinion leaders of various social worlds have tended to focus on this integrating activity.

While only a few of the older people interviewed were engaged in marketing, many were active organizers at various levels within social worlds. Once again, Henry Farley represents the most obvious example. Not only was he the founding parent of the gleaning world, but he continued to supply the energy and knowledge that held it together. At a lower level within the same social world, Thelma Harding (Figure 3.4) had invested considerable energy toward the organization of food pickups and produce distribution to charities and other gleaners. Her location at the apex of the telephone tree is further evidence of her immersion in this activity.

In a comparative sense, however, Thelma Harding was not as deeply integrated nor as fully immersed in gleaning as Henry Farley. Thelma's organizing activities were not located as near the core of the gleaning world as those of Henry. Further, Henry had combined organizing activities with marketing, creating, and consuming. In addition, he was engaged in the next activity to be discussed, which facilitated even deeper integration. By necessity, then, his activities situated him at the heart of that social world. Therefore, the evaluation of social integration requires not only awareness of which integrating activity was assumed, but the combination of multiple activities as well. It is also important to reiterate that most of the organizing activities assumed by the older people interviewed were located in worlds with high proportions of elderly participants. These were also the worlds where marketing and rigid evaluations of participants were downplayed. For the most part, the elderly participants felt such matters encouraged unnecessary competition and insecurity. They had lived much of their lives in the face of such matters and sought more tranquility. For example, there was resistance among elderly ballroom dancers to any kind of competition that would determine the best dancers, most attractive couple, or oldest active participants.

Representing

The act of *representing* other social world participants provides another avenue of integration. It is an activity that situates people very near the core of vital activities, processes, and events. Representing implies that those involved are serving as agents and advocates for the ideas, concerns, and problems of others. At the lowest level, there are those who represent colleagues in meetings of various circles or subworlds. That is, the business at hand probably would focus on matters internal to the specific social world. In other words, representatives at this level generally would not be concerned with the legitimization of the broad focus of their social world, whether it be baseball, classical music, square dancing, or bowling. Instead, they would focus on resolving differences with regard to internal orientations, attitudes, and stances toward the focus of their social worlds. In addition, representatives at this level engage in recruitment of new participants and plot new directions for participants. There are, however, representatives who operate at higher levels. These people serve as agents and advocates for social world interests in much larger contexts. For example, representatives from the worlds of business, real estate, government, and the like may meet with those from old age groups, senior centers, churches, voluntary associations, and neighborhood groups to resolve the problem of elderly housing. Anselm Strauss (1978b) has used the term *arenas* to refer to the contexts and locations where representatives of social worlds, interest groups, formal organizations, voluntary associations, and territorial communities meet to negotiate social problems (see Wiener, 1981).

While those who represent the interests of social worlds in various arenas probably have somewhat greater knowledge than those who operate at lower levels, all representatives must have intimate familiarity with the desires, intentions, prospects, problems, and prospects of those for whom they speak. Of the many older people interviewed, only Henry Farley could be viewed as a representative. In this instance, representing went hand in hand with organizing the activities and marketing the products of the gleaners. Henry routinely represented the gleaners at meetings, which included agents for community gardening groups, food banks, senior centers, food coops, and stores. Involvement in these meetings served to increase the influence of Henry Farley and the gleaners. Jack and Gwen Hurling (Figure 3.2), on the other hand, had once represented their local square dancing group at conventions up and down the West Coast. However, these activities were accomplished when they were much younger. Their absence from that world for several years due to Jack's heart attack effectively removed them from any integrating activity that would immerse them as deeply as representing once had. Instead, the simple performance of square dancing became paramount in their minds.

It is necessary to reemphasize that this activity, perhaps more than any other, has located people at the very core of various social worlds. Those who serve as representatives must have access to knowledge and information unavailable to most participants. As with marketing, an affiliation with a formal organization seems to provide an entree and access to such activity. Therefore, as the experiences of the older people interviewed have demonstrated, retirement has removed the aging from this activity. It was highly unlikely that a younger or age-mixed world would seek representation from an elderly person. Also, representing is an activity demanding much from those who would be involved. Many of the older people expressed no desire to expend the energy, time, and effort that would have been required even if they had been offered the opportunity to represent the interests of others.

Evaluating

A final avenue for social world integration involves the judging and assessment of the objects, products, performances, creations, marketing, and representation of others. *Evaluating,* then, is an activity that involves only a very small proportion of those involved. These are the few people whose opinions and judgments are disseminated widely among the rest of social world members. The roles of critic, reviewer, editor, judge, referee, inspector, and assessor involve a great deal of evaluating. As a means of social integration, it demands

detailed knowledge of the complex issues, standards, and requirements which social worlds devise. It also requires, for the most part,
the practical knowledge of when the rigid standards should be invoked and when they might be ignored or downplayed.

Even more than organizing and representing, evaluating is something people become immersed in only after long periods of time in
other activities. In effect, they must pay their dues and work their
way into such positions. While it is likely that there are aged critics,
reviewers, and judges in various social worlds, none arose in the
many interviews with older people. In partial explanation, it must be
noted that evaluating often evolves out of relationships and positions
in formal organizations, voluntary associations, and interest groups.
Should positions in these forms of social organization be lost through
a variety of circumstances, so too would the role of evaluator be lost.
Also, as previously implied, many worlds with a high proportion of
elderly participants quite consciously downplayed the importance of
judging and assessing the contributions of those who would be involved. Instead, a high premium was placed on mere participation
and personal enjoyment. It generally was felt that a critical or
judgmental stance would discourage involvement and risk-taking
among those less sure of their abilities and the attitudes of others.
Finally, it must be reiterated that the rapid social change associated
with this form of social organization also implies constantly changing
ideas, standards, and procedures. It is, therefore, very difficult for an
evaluator of any age to keep up with changes of many kinds. To some
degree, there may exist a generation gap within social worlds by
which older participants seek to maintain the standards and procedures relevant when they began their careers, with younger participants seeking to institute new practices and systems of evaluation.
Such conflict is reminiscent of that described by Vern Bengston and
Joseph Kuypers (1971) in their general discussion of the generation
gap. The essential tension between the older and younger generations
seems to be between continuity and emergence. The older generation
seeks to maintain many beliefs, practices, and ideas that influenced
them in their youth, while younger people seek self-discovery and
social experimentation. There is every reason to believe this tension
exists in all areas of social life — including social worlds.

AGE-RELATED INFLUENCES

In this section the focus shifts away from factors internal to social worlds that affected the nature and degree of social integration among the aged. Instead, the purpose of this discussion is to step back from the social and psychological experiences of older people and focus on the influence of various external forces on their lives in specific social worlds. Time and again, the interviews with older people revealed the importance of economic resources, physical condition, family status, and residential location on the experiences of the individual aged. These factors are external in the sense that their presence or absence was beyond the direct control of the older individuals. That is, much as many of them may have wished to change their basic cir-cumstances along any one of these dimensions, most were powerless to do so. On the other hand, most older people sought to construct their daily lives so as to minimize and control the influence of these factors. These efforts will be highlighted in this discussion.

It is also important to note that these external forces may also be seen as somewhat age-related. The gerontological literature is marked by references to these factors, which refer to them as char-acteristics of old age and elderly people.[1] Declining economic re-sources, potentially drastic changes in physical condition, alterations in family status, and residential relocation very much characterize old age when compared with experiences of middle age (Bultena and Wood, 1969; Cumming and Henry, 1961; Hochschild, 1978; Johnson, 1971; Rosow, 1967, 1974; Simpson and McKinney, 1966). Of course, individually these factors influence the lives of many younger and middle-aged people. However, in combination, they characterize the lives of a good proportion of elderly people.

Economic Resources

It especially was true that economic resources influenced the specific social worlds into which the older people were integrated, as well as the kinds of activities performed. Most lived on fixed incomes or meager pensions that seemed to cover only basic necessities. While the majority of them were not poor, they did have to apportion their finances carefully each month to cover their food, housing, and medical expenses. Still, a relatively broad range of economic situations existed among the older people portrayed in this study. Quite obviously Henry Farley, the retired stockbroker, was fairly comfortable in retirement, as were the Petersons after Robert's many years with a major banking firm. Relative economic well-being allowed both parties to set aside the pragmatic concerns of day-to-day living so they could focus on other concerns. For example, to Robert and Sarah Peterson, the Phoenix art world became the object of much attention — in addition to the world of internees.

Broadly speaking, there was a tendency for social class to be a strong influence on the kinds of social worlds in which the aged were involved. It was most apparent that involvement of the Petersons in the world of art and the activities they performed reflected class interests. They were matched with other art-lovers who shared their income and interests. In addition, there was a strong norm of volunteerism among their colleagues in Phoenix. That is, their participation was not focused toward direct economic gain, but rather on civic involvement and personal satisfaction. Involvement in the worlds of classical music, ballet, bowling, and automobile racing may very well be based on interests and perspectives located in social class.

In addition, economic resources affected the ways by which the aged were engaged in various worlds. Clearly, if Fred Romano had not been a retired State of California employee with a comfortable pension, he could not have been as active and instrumental in the bicycling world. When seriously pursued, bicycling is an expensive avocation requiring substantial economic investments. Different kinds of events require bicycles of varying weights, materials, durability, and gearing. Fred owned three bicycles for the touring and shorter races. In total, his investment was well over $2000. Further, he personally financed a number of cross-country and European tours that required substantial outlays for transportation and lodging. Had Fred Romano been less economically secure, it is doubtful he could have engaged in the same events that eventually made him well known in many states and countries.

Perhaps more interesting and sociologically important are the aged who have scrimped and saved simply to cover basic necessities. Exemplary of this condition, Arnold and Jean Goodrich (Figure 1.2) had a combined monthly income of less than $600. They lived in a mobile home in a working-class trailer court and generally had developed social involvements consistent with their economic position. The local senior center, informal bridge groups, and family involvements all could be pursued with a minimum capital outlay and very little extra for continued activity. Through involvement at the senior center, they became aware of the local bowling scene for seniors. Bowling was something they had not done and they believed it would be a good source of exercise, concentration, and sociability. Therefore, they went to a nearby Goodwill store and found two bowling balls, carrying bags, and pairs of suitable shoes for a total economic investment of $2.49. While they had to spend small amounts of money each time they bowled, it was inconsequential when compared to the costs of other activities.

In a very real sense, the Goodrichs selected a social world and integrating activity that could be pursued with a minimum economic investment. However, during the high inflation of the early 1980s, Arnold and Jean also found themselves giving up a lifelong dream of extensive world travel. For many years, they had hoped to see Europe and the homes of their ancestors. In addition, the tight squeeze of inflation curbed a certain amount of involvement with their family. Since their children lived in places up and down the West Coast, it was difficult for them to visit as often as they wished. Interestingly, the Goodrichs did not see themselves as deprived, but rather doing the best they could under trying circumstances. They said they often talked about which of their many social involvements they would give up if their situation became worse. In effect, they were strategizing as to how they could operate within their economic constraints with no relief in sight. The following comment by Jean nicely illustrates their attitude.

> Well, when you're in our situation — and I think you'll find a lot of people who are like us — well, you learn to dwell in your own realm of capabilities. If inflation gets much worse, we would cut back even more on groceries and the car. . . . But I hope I wouldn't ever have to give up my bowling.

The place of bowling in their lives was certainly indicated by Jean's apparent willingness to cut back on food expenses and sell their automobile. Whether or not they truly would have given these things up for the sake of bowling is not important, but rather the mere thought of such sacrifices for bowling reveals their priorities.

Finally, the gleaning world represented a collective effort on the part of the aged to combat the economic insecurities of old age. It represents, in fact, a world that provided economic benefits to all involved. Thelma and Thomas Harding (Figure 3.4) were not particularly fond of scrounging for forgotten produce in the hot and dusty fields of Northern California. However, the effort was necessary for them to obtain quality foodstuffs with minimal economic investment. Another factor which made gleaning economically rewarding for the elderly was their reluctance to place a dollar value on their time. Most had large stretches of free time they were willing to devote to physical labor. If they had to take time off from work or other more economically rewarding pursuits, gleaning for charitable and personal use would not have been rewarding.

There were several older people who managed to transform a leisure pursuit into one that was economically rewarding. Those in the worlds of art, photography, antiques, old automobiles, and stamp collecting are good examples of people combining expressive and instrumental goals.

Physical Condition

The stereotype depicting older people as frail and unhealthy holds some truth, but wide interpersonal variations existed among the older people in this study. Clearly, not everyone fit the stereotype, nor handled their infirmities in the same manner (see Matthews, 1979; Shanas, 1962, 1970). It was apparent, however, that older people were more susceptible to certain conditions, and that the retarded healing process brought about through advancing age made life problematic. The elderly involved in accidents or illnesses tended to be plagued by the conditions for many years after. While their younger counterparts probably would have recovered in several weeks or months, these older people had to confront these chronic conditions for many years. The example of Lucy Anderson (Figure 2.2) exemplifies this notion. To recount her situation, Lucy was struck by a passing van, at the age of 82, while walking home from the supermarket. Her injured hip became chronically painful and eventually forced her out of the ballroom dancing world. She simply could not muster the stamina or movement to engage in dancing as she once had. Her movements necessarily were cautious and unsure. Coupled with intense pain and the fear of further injury, Lucy reluctantly stopped attending dances. The other end of the continuum, of course, is represented by Fred Romano whose excellent health and conditioning helped make him an exemplar in bicycling. In fact, his good health and pride surely must have helped his recovery from the broken leg he received during a bicycling event. The relationship between physical condition and the experiences of these two elderly individuals is clear and straightforward.

However, it is a mistake to assume a simple correlation between good physical condition and satisfying social world integration. Several others used the onset of physical illnesses, disabilities, or conditions as benchmarks signaling the beginning or end of various involvements. That is, the onset of heart attacks, strokes, accidents, or paralyses segmented their lives into precrisis and postcrisis social activities. Of course, it was not the physical condition alone that governed the course upon which these older people embarked, rather, it was how the crisis was incorporated and managed as part of their identities (Davis, 1963).

Jack Hurling's heart attack was a crisis that thrust him and his wife into social isolation (Figure 3.2). It was earlier described that this condition forced early retirement on him and that Gwen quit her secretarial job to nurse him back to health. Most relevant to this discussion is how Jack's chronic heart condition affected their reintegration into the world of square dancing. At one point in the interview, Jack described the physical problems experienced after the heart attack, at home, and the first few times he tried to dance.

> I have to get circulation in my legs or they go numb. My fingers . . . the circulation there is poor and if I overdo myself, my breathing is labored. . . . We used to square dance quite a bit, but stopped over sixteen years ago. But now we are getting back into it. At the cannery, it was seven days a week work, and the first few years I worked twelve hours a day. Needless to say, you just don't feel much like square dancing when you get home at night. We went back one time a year or so ago. Some friends of ours were dancing over at the Catholic church and they called us up and said, "Hey, what are you kids doing tonight?" They needed another couple for the class they were teaching, and so we went. I hadn't danced since my heart attack, but I thought I could handle it. I walk around the trailer court here twice a day and I think I have built up my condition pretty

good. You know, when I came home from the hospital, I walked up those three steps over there and I thought I would never make it up. They seemed to be about ten feet high and a mile apart. That walking several miles a day has really helped me, I think. That kind of thing should be good for getting used to square dancing again. . . . At any rate, the first time back dancing I had to go very slow and take my time. The other people were real understanding and slowed down to make room for me. When we go back more regularly, I know we will have to watch it more closely than I did before. . . . I was just so glad to get back out there. . . .

The major change, then, for Jack and Gwen Hurling seemed to be the constant worry and monitoring of his condition. Gwen, perhaps even more than Jack, believed she paid more attention to his physical condition and symptoms.

While Jack Hurling made no claim that square dancing was therapeutic, another older person embarked upon a social world career for exactly that reason. The nature of involvement and the kind of activity performed was quite different than Jack Hurling's dancing. This older woman became more deeply immersed in the art world specifically because it was recommended that painting might improve her eye/hand coordination. These problems were the result of an auto accident in which the woman suffered severe brain damage. Interestingly, the accident and disability significantly altered her family life and emotional stability, while thrusting her more deeply into the art world. The separation and eventual divorce that closely followed the accident left her with vast amounts of unstructured time that had to be filled by therapeutic activities.

Family Status

A third influence on the nature and degree of integration into social worlds relates to matters of family status. This broad category includes three components: (1) the presence or absence of a spouse or significant other; (2) proximity of children; and (3) living situation, which would include extended families, retirement communities, neighborhoods, and living alone. In conversation with older people, it quickly became apparent that perhaps the most crucial component related to the presence or absence of significant others. Not only did the presence of a significant other provide an entree to various involvements, but it also supplied certain older people with allies in their social world careers.[2] Clearly, Alice Romano was extremely influential in facilitating her husband's bicycling career and, most important, in providing support and encouragement as he convalesced after his broken leg. According to both parties, time and again Fred expressed the belief that he might never have returned to active bicycling if it were not for Alice's constant encouragement and cajoling. The presence of joint activities among the other older couples in this study is further testimony to the importance of allies.

The absence of a spouse or significant other further influenced which social worlds arose and became relevant to the lives of certain older people. Implicitly or explicitly, many social activities functioned as places where single, widowed, or divorced older people could meet others in the same situations. Erma Martin (Figure 2.4) most readily comes to mind in this context. Much of her social life was devoted to situating herself in the company of single older men. She evaluated many social worlds and other involvements according to the probabilities for meeting interesting men. Therefore, she consciously chose not to attend certain kinds of meetings, undertake certain activities, or engage in some events because the odds were against her. At one point in the interview, she remarked that the local senior center never had interested her for these reasons.

> I just have never really gotten myself involved down there. Well, mostly there are almost no men down there, or even at many of the activities they sponsor. I mean that's an important part of life. At least you want to go down there and see an occasional man. Of course, there are a few who go down there for lunches and other things. Unfortunately, they are either too old, I mean too old for me, or they go down there with their wives. You know, sometimes it gets a little depressing down there. If I didn't know better, I would think that this town had only married men and men who don't really have a whole lot going for them. You know, they don't really have the same interests that I do. . . .

While there may have been other people who evaluated involvements according to the same criteria, Erma was the most vocal about her approach. She felt alone and sought to do something about it.

Children, grandchildren, and extended families were further influences on the nature and degree of social world involvements. Nearly all of the people interviewed lived reasonably near at least one of their children. This reflected the situation of older people in general, of whom it is said two-thirds either share a household with a child, or live within a ten-minutes drive (Shanas, 1970, 1980). Most of the older people spent considerable time with their children and grandchildren, considering it an important component of everyday life. Of the forty people interviewed, nearly half had relocated after retirement to be nearer their children. For the most part, they felt the relocation beneficial and moved at the insistence of their children.

For Robert and Sarah Peterson, relocation from Phoenix to be near their daughter meant forsaking deep immersion in the art world for rather superficial and peripheral involvement via the media. In conversation, the Petersons recognized the costs and benefits of their relocation and accepted them.

> Then when our daughter seemed to settle here permanently, we thought it would be a good place to settle. We can manage pretty good here. As time goes on, we don't need to have a place where we can be more active than we are at the present time. Yet, in some respects, living here has not been as satisfactory as life in the Phoenix area. We had a lot of connections there that made life a little easier and more worthwhile. As you now know, through some friends in Arizona, I had become interested in the art museum and all the activities of those people. We had become part of that group and participated and initiated activities there. In fact, most of our friends were active in the museum too. Some still are even though they are about as old as we are. Even though we still keep up with things going on in art, it just isn't the same as it once was.

Continued involvement in the family clearly was more important to most of the older people than integration into other forms of social organization. While they would have preferred not having to make a choice between involvements, their priorities were set. This leads to the final factor, which very much relates to the previous ones. The presence or absence of significant others, as well as family situations, greatly influenced the residential locations of the aged.

Residential Area

The relocation of Robert and Alice Peterson from Arizona to Northern California hints at the potential impact of residential area on ntegration into social worlds. By leaving the Phoenix area, the Petersons were removed from the art subworld into which they had been deeply immersed. They found themselves out of the core network of activities, events, organizations, and processes into which many of their friends had been integrated. Therefore, a significant change in residential location drastically altered the kind of integrating activity they assumed in the larger art world. Of course, changes in residential location have also immersed older people more deeply into various worlds. Some older stamp collectors described by Edwin Christ (1965) consciously moved to cities such as Miami, Los Angeles, and Seattle that had developed reputations as important centers for philatelic activity. In essence, these cities containing dealers, collectors, publishers, and distributors had developed into regional subworlds. They had become the cores of networks that spread outward to participants, connected through one of their many linking devices.

Clearly, people do not become immersed in the activities of social worlds simply by moving into certain regions, territories, cities, or neighborhoods. However, these movements may facilitate immersion into networks, which is later transformed into the cognitive identification so necessary for social world integration. The origins of the gleaning world and the presence of willing and able older people had much to do with residential area. Were it not for their location in the prime agricultural region of California, it is doubtful that gleaning would have become a viable social world involvement. Also, had a large body of activist and concerned older people not been concentrated in the same region, gleaning might not have mushroomed into the widespread, well-developed, and functioning world it has become for the aged.

The other effects of residential area on integration into social worlds are many. Relocation into a nursing home or convalescent hospital effectively may remove older people from contact with the concerns of social worlds in which they once had been involved. It is not that continued integration into those concerns would be impossible, but that these institutions are not structured to facilitate continued involvement. For example, rigid work routines and exclusive concern with feeding, dressing, and managing patients would discourage assistance to residents seeking to maintain interests via letter writing, journal subscriptions, and the like (Gubrium, 1975). Similarly, movement into a retirement community or village might situate older people away from core activities in subworlds of various kinds. It might, then, be more difficult to maintain the contacts necessary for continuing activities providing satisfactory integration.

The integrating activities introduced and explored in this chapter imply crucial changes in perspective, knowledge, and perception as older people move more deeply in to (or out of) the whirlpool of activities in specific social worlds. Using this discussion of integrating activities and age-related factors as background, the following chapter focuses on the phenomenology of elderly involvement. That is, attention is given to changes in experience as the older people serving as major characters in this study moved in to, through, and out of various social worlds.

NOTES

1. The following sources will provide specific details regarding some of the age-related influences discussed in this section. With regard to physical condition and its effects on social involvement in old age, see Brody (1973), Butler and Lewis (1973), Shanas and Maddox (1976), Wilder (1971, 1973). The effects of declining economic resources on the social lives of the aged are well covered by Campbell (1977), Munnell (1977), and Schulz (1980). While retirement was not specifically discussed as a separate category of age-related factors, its affects widely are recognized by Atchley (1976), Friedmann and Orbach (1974), Simpson and McKinney (1966), Streib (1974), Wilensky (1961). Finally, as earlier described, widowhood and the loss of others very close to older people may have dramatic effects on social integration. See Atchley (1975), Charmaz (1980), Glick et al. (1974), Lopata (1973), and Marshall (1980).

2. In her discussion of managing the dying role, Lyn Lofland (1978: 67) notes the impact of surrounding others on the ways the dying shape the role. The presence of a supportive ally may allow the dying to engage in activities that would be unavailable to them in other circumstances. Similarly, the absence of foes may allow the fulfillment of wishes and desires that might be illegal, unethical, or immoral. The effects of surrounding others on social world involvement probably are similar, if less dramatic.

5

TYPES OF SOCIAL WORLD INTEGRATION

Throughout this study, it has been noted that roles in social worlds are characterized by high degrees of informality. That is, people may identify with the perspectives, concerns, and issues of various worlds without explicit acknowledgement by other participants. Movement in and out of these spheres of influence may be relatively easy. The only crucial factor for minimal social world involvement is access to one of many linking devices. It was noted earlier that the structure of social worlds facilitates and encourages the invisible presence of participants. At this point it is helpful to restate three important points. First, the very large population subsumed within social worlds makes the presence or absence of individuals unfelt. As with all social actors, older people tend to be part of many hundreds or thousands of other people involved. Second, those who are involved probably are dispersed over vast territories. This is the effect of mass media and other channels of communication. Therefore, cognitive identification and not formal membership, bureaucratic roles, territorial delimiters, or ascribed traits tend to define the boundaries. Finally, a high degree of permeability and relatively weak authority structures are the end products of spatial dispersion. Consequently, entry into most social worlds is poorly controlled. Measures to facilitate or discourage entry probably are most effective at lower levels in subworlds or social circles.

With the highly informal character of social involvement in mind, this chapter focuses on the types of involvement, or stances people tend to assume within social worlds. These types are more complex than the integrating activities described in the previous chapter. Rather than focusing on the means by which people maintain linkages, the social types to be developed are formal abstractions encapsulating the everyday experiences of people in various social worlds. The generalized experiences of older people in social worlds, then, will be codified and analyzed according to a scheme of four social types.[1] These four types, or stances, describe important differences among people as they move more deeply into the structure of specific social worlds. *Strangers, tourists, regulars,* and *insiders* are terms signifying positions occupied by people in relation to the whirlpool of knowledge, activities, events, and processes swirling about those things that have brought people together. At one level, the scheme of social types conceptualizes important differences among people of all ages within social worlds. However, at another level, they are relevant for understanding some of the dynamics of aged involvement.

The chapter is organized around the scheme of social types, beginning with those that describe the experiences of people located outside the boundaries of social worlds. The progression to be discussed, then, is that of people moving more deeply into the structure of the social organizational form. While the set of social types implies logical and orderly progression toward the core of various social worlds, this was not the case in everyday life. Most people did not progress through more than one or two social types. Only a very small number ever reached the role of insider. In drawing generalizations about aged integration, the orientations, experiences, relationships, and commitment of older people in each stage will be discussed.

STRANGERS

In his essay on the stranger, Georg Simmel (1950) noted how those located outside certain social groups might be considered full-fledged members. This was so because strangers defined the boundaries of these groups by their mere presence, and represented a population toward which many group activities had to be directed. For example, social groups of all kinds must decide whom to exclude and include in their activities. In short, those who were not strangers were, by definition, part of the group. The notion of strangers in various contexts has been of interest to many theorists since Simmel. Margaret Mary Wood (1934) emphasized the social relationsips of people who found themselves in this role. In fact, the transience and marginality associated with this social type has made it a catchword for the perceived impersonality and alienation of modern social life.

In terms of imagery, the writings of Alfred Schutz (1944) have been the most useful. He conceived strangers as existing at the outer edges of social groups and communities where knowledge was organized into "stratified layers of relevance." In effect, the metaphor was that of a contour map in which social knowledge, personal meaning, and perception increases as people move more deeply into these contexts. This imagery is reminiscent of the whirlpool metaphor I have used to describe the organization of social worlds. In a sense, then, strangers must be conceived as existing at the outer edges or boundaries of social worlds, even though they routinely are taken into account by those more deeply integrated. Attempts by social world participants to recruit, acknowledge, or exclude strangers confirm their location at this point.

Most important for the study of the aged in social worlds is the idea that all participants must once have been strangers. This stance or social type represents the point of departure for everyone who eventually moved more deeply into the spheres of influence of various social worlds. This discussion is organized around four qualities that describe the essence of this social type (1) *naïveté* in their orientation toward social world relationships and activities; (2) personal experiences largely characterized by *disorientation* and confusion; (3) relationships with participants that are *superficial* at best; and (4) a great deal of *detachment* from the on-going concerns of these social worlds, resulting in very little commitment.

Naïveté

In the view of Schutz (1944: 502), strangers tend to interpret their experiences in new contexts and environments according to background knowledge developed in other contexts. In effect, when strangers come into contact with the activities, events, processes, and organizations of various social worlds, they naively apply a system of relevance that has allowed them to understand other situations. Their unfamiliar experiences, then, may or may not be made comprehensible in this manner. The practices and procedures developed in one social world may be similar enough to the new experiences of strangers to be useful in making sense of the experience. However, there are other times when this practice may only confuse or frustrate the people involved. In his study of taxi-dance halls in Chicago during the 1920s and 1930s, Paul Cressey discovered how the practice of applying an established system of relevance to a new experience could reveal to other participants that a stranger was in their midst. In the following excerpt, note how a veteran dancer immediately recognized Cressey, the sociologist as a stranger to the taxi-dance hall world.

> The first time I saw you, I knew right away you didn't belong on West Madison Street. You didn't act like the other white fellows who came up the hill. . . . You'd even go up and talk straight out to the boss, but none of the others would have done that until they'd known him. . . . Then when you'd come over to me, you'd ask me to dance — not just hand me a ticket like the others (Cressey, 1932: 25).

It is through interaction with people integrated into various social worlds that people realize the system of relevance they brought with them does not help them understand what is going on, feel more comfortable in their surroundings, or become more deeply integrated. Importantly, several of the older people interviewed remarked about situations wherein they felt uncomfortable and reticent. However, most of them did not really know why they felt the way they did. To be sure, many were confronted with beliefs and practices that did not make much sense. For example, Lucy Anderson (Figure 2.2) noted how some friends tried to interest her in the activity of collecting in several social worlds. As the following excerpt illustrates, she simply did not understand these worlds and did not wish to try.

> One of my friends here in the apartments keeps trying to get me to go to these shows they always have in shopping centers for people who

collect all sorts of things. You know, people who collect Avon bottles, postcards, and stuff like that. I did go with her once, but I didn't really think much of it. I didn't enjoy the day a whole lot. Besides, to me most of these things are just junk and hardly worth the trouble.

Trying new things is difficult for many people. However, for some of the older people, finding new frontiers seemed especially troublesome. Some, like Lucy Anderson, had been blocked from active involvement in worlds that appealed to them, while others simply did not want to spend their old age in a state of confusion, ambiguity, and uncertainty. These feelings most certainly would have been present if they actively entered the domains of many alien social worlds. For the most part, it simply was too comfortable to remain in familiar domains.

Disorientation

Like Lucy Anderson, most people have come into contact with social worlds whereupon they immediately were confronted with the sense of being strangers. The naïveté which led them to assume that former systems of relevance applied to new social worlds may also stimulate feelings of disorientation. That is, they were unsure about matters of procedure, protocol, demeanor, and the like. Not knowing what is going on, nor what to expect from other participants, has been a common experience for strangers. These feelings of disorientation were apparent in the uneasiness of the older people in such situations. For some, these experiences were enough to keep them from ever thinking about further integration.

Disorientation has also resulted in unwitting violations of social world rules and procedures. These violations, when discovered, have led to an even greater exaggeration of these feelings. In illustration, Lucy Anderson went on to remark about her uncomfortable feelings when she told her friend that bottle collecting did not interest her. Apparently, her friend became somewhat defensive and began offering justifications for collecting what Lucy had termed worthless junk. Lucy had not realized she was questioning or perhaps attacking the very foundation of that world. In essence, only through the violation of this social world's norms did she become aware of their existence.

Examples of disorientation found in the lives of two other older people were less traumatic for them. Most important, feelings of disorientation seemed to discourage any attempts for further integration into those worlds.

Superficiality

Relationships between strangers and those more deeply integrated tend to be superficial, transitory, and fleeting. In fact, it is almost by definition that strangers no longer can be considered such when relationships have moved beyond this point. The shared perspectives and interests that link those involved in the same social world do not exist between strangers and others. While it is possible for strangers to have close personal ties to those within certain social worlds, the link will be along lines other than those that would bind them into those worlds. For example, Lucy Anderson's friendship with the bottle collector obviously was formed and maintained in other contexts.   .

It also is important to note that many strangers have not desired nor sought deeper integration into many worlds.[2] Quite simply, most of the older people who perceived themselves as strangers had not sought greater involvement. The relatively few times when they left this position and tried to move more deeply into the sphere of influence of a specific social world, it was because they had detected a note of relevance in the activities for their lives. Movement out of this role is, as it will later be elaborated, more difficult than simply expressing a desire to do so. A certain amount of receptivity among social world participants must be found. They must, if only in a small way, be willing to provide information about rules, procedures, and access to linking devices. Access to information about social world activities is crucial to movement out of this stance.

Detachment

Based on the other characteristics of this stance, it is apparent that strangers have little commitment to the on-going concerns of social worlds with which they have had contact. Once again, by definition, strangers are detached from the everyday concerns that might plague or excite those more deeply integrated. Alfred Schutz (1944) used the term "doubtful loyalty" to describe the commitment of strangers to the concerns of any group or community. Similarly, Robert Park (1937) and Everett Stonequist (1937) spoke about the "marginal man" in similar contexts. Most important, it is the location of strangers on the periphery of social worlds that allows them a high degree of objectivity or, perhaps, indifference toward that which has consumed the lives of others. Therefore, some of the beliefs, practices, and ideologies that seem quite normal to social world participants may be viewed as strange, exotic, curious, or objectionable by strangers. Once again, Lucy Anderson could not understand why anyone would devote considerable time, effort, and expense toward the collection of bottles and jars. In her mind, they were not pretty to look at, nor did they seem to have much economic value.

TOURISTS

A second stance that places people more deeply into the concerns of various social worlds is what might be termed the *tourist*. Generally, the term has been used to describe people who have embarked upon journeys for pleasure, culture, or even simple diversion (Boorstin, 1961; MacCannell, 1973, 1976; Turner and Ash, 1975). With regard to social world involvement, the term encapsulates the stance of a good proportion of participants. Tourists are people who enter the domains of social worlds in search of a certain kind of experience. They want to see, feel, and understand typical processes, activities, and events. For example, tourists in the art world might seek to understand how particular works were created, the idiosyncracies of the artist that influenced the product, and knowledge of the evaluation system.

Compared with strangers, tourists clearly have penetrated the boundaries of social worlds. They have entered these spheres of influence and have begun to learn the rules, vocabularies, and attitudes peculiar to those worlds. The tourist stance, then, is the next logical step taken by strangers seeking deeper integration. Even though the worlds that tourists have entered must have been relevant, receptive, and accessible, they largely remain at the outer edges of the whirlpool structure. For example, when relating this stance with integrating activities, it is likely tourists would move into the role through consuming. By consuming the products, activities, and processes constructed by others, these people would take their first steps toward more intimate familiarity. While tourists might also engage in collecting, creating, and performing, it is likely most of their efforts would be focused on consumption. Movement toward the core of social worlds requires interest, concern, and dedication tourists might not want to expend. However, it is also important to remember that this stance may, for a limited number of participants, be a way-station toward greater involvement.

The tourist role is extremely important for understandng the experiences of large numbers of older people. It will become apparent that a sizeable number of older people mentioned in earlier chapters must be characterized as tourists. With this in mind, there are four qualities that describe the essence of the tourist role: (1) an orientation toward the concerns of social worlds marked by *curiosity;* (2) most experiences with the activities and process of social worlds are aimed at *learning;* (3) relationships with other participants that are *transient* as tourists move through seeking new experiences; and (4) commitment to the functioning of social worlds only when involvement has *entertainment* value.

Curiosity

The inclination to learn more about what is going on within social worlds is the orientation of tourists. Curiosity, then, is an important motivator for greater involvement and deeper integration. This orientation is crucial for movement from the role of stranger to tourist. For example, Fred Romano (Figure 3.1) had not been on a bicycle for over forty years when, just prior to his retirement, he saw a single touring bicyclist in the Sierra Nevada. In effect, Fred had been a stranger to the bicycling world for a very long period of time. The sight of the bicyclist sparked memories of the past and stimulated his curiosity about contemporary bicycling and his retirement. In his words,

> At around the age of 58, that was in 1963, I saw a guy touring up in the Sierra. I was on one of my inspection trips and I said, "By golly, that sure looks interesting." I hadn't ridden a bicycle since high school, but I sure wanted to take that up again. So I talked to him about all the equipment he had. I was trying to see what kind of

equipment I might need to get back into bicycling. . . . You know, if I hadn't talked to him, I probably would have just run out and bought a Sears bicycle. Eventually, I bought myself a pretty good bicycle.

Fred's curiosity about changes in technology, equipment, and practices was the basis for his encounter with the bicyclist and, to a large degree, steered him in the right direction. That is, it was his desire to learn which products were legitimate and authentic that cleared the path for fairly rapid integration. He began his bicycling career, then, without having to flounder about learning the very basics of that world. For the most part, however, tourists tend not to be as forthright as Fred Romano. Many simply wish to view and vicariously experience the activities of others. In this way, their fantasies or desires are fulfilled without risking the humiliation of performing, creating, or whatever.

Learning

The process of learning more about what social worlds are about characterizes the experiences of tourists. In this way, these consumers seek to increase their familiarity with the processes and activities that might thrust them more deeply into the concerns of these worlds. In short, a considerable portion of tourists' effort is consumed by the near constant activity of becoming oriented to the distinct practices, procedures, evaluation systems, and the like generated by social worlds. Whether or not the process of learning these things thrusts tourists more deeply into those worlds, isolates them in the role, or encourages movement out of the spheres of influence depends upon the combination of personal desires, age-related factors, proportion of older people involved, and other factors previously explored. If people have been granted access to the linking devices, subworlds, and personalities within, they likely would move into one or more of the other stances.

Transiency

However, while still tourists, the relationships of people within social worlds are highly transitory and fleeting. Like the typical tourist in everyday life, those in specific social worlds tend to sample life at the activities, events, and processes conducted by others. In one sense, social world tourists tend not to seek nor desire sustained relationships with others. If they did, they more than likely would begin movement into other roles which would bring them closer to the core of social world activities. Transient relationships are typical because, by their nature, tourists probably would move on to other social worlds in a matter hours, days, or perhaps weeks. Sustained involvement through good times and bad is nonexistent. In short, tourists in the worlds of art, music, dance, or whatever tend to be those who have become only superficially aware of complex issues and ideas. As a result, they have little in common with art critics or ballet afficionados who speak a language they do not understand, judge performances in ways they do not comprehend, and travel in circles to which tourists are excluded.

Entertainment

Finally, largely as a result of the other qualities, tourists demonstrate very little commitment to the existence of social worlds. Perhaps more than anything else, they are interested and involved only when things are going well. Should adversity arise, it is likely tourists would drop their involvement and move on. For example, should conflict among subworlds arise regarding the tone and direction of future activities, it is likely tourists would avoid the debates to pursue more comfortable activities elsewhere. Significant expenditures of time, energy, and interest are not characteristic of these participants. Instead, they seek only limited understanding. In illustration, Anselm Strauss (1961: 68-81) has urged city dwellers to adopt the "touristic attitude" by which they explore and appreciate social worlds hidden in their own cities. Strauss has noted that urbanites might then appreciate and understand the immense diversity and heterogeneity characteristic of city life. Implicit in the definition, then, is the emphasis on on personal entertainment. When the desired experience is achieved, if it becomes too burdensome, or even if it simply is no longer interesting, tourists move on to other worlds.

Most important to this study, a good many of the older people interviewed must be characterized as tourists. It was a stance often consciously and forthrightly adopted as they sought relief from the pressures, demands, and commitments of their middle years. In varying degrees, most of them expressed sentiments like the following.

I've really had it with having to be somewhere at a particular time. After I retired, I decided that I would just do whatever I pleased for awhile. . . . For me that means being able to sleep as late as I want, and not having to be someplace, or do something at a certain time. . . .

I haven't really found much that keeps my interest up since my husband died. I sort of try a little of this for awhile, and then a little of that. I just seem to lose interest after not too long. . . . Pretty soon, something else seems to come along and catch my eye. I might then do it for awhile and give it some time. Still, you know, I'm not too willing to use much of my free time for extracurricular activities. . . . I like to just pop in for a short time.

Clearly, of all the major characters in this study, Erma Martin (Figure 2.4) was the quintessential tourist. She adopted the stance in nearly all social involvements. Only her commitment to the family escaped the transience of her interest. In her profile, it is apparent that she found herself moving out of the worlds of ballroom dancing, gleaning, and the bowling group while moving into church involvement and a bridge group. Learning about these activities, satisfying her curiosity, and deriving entertainment were ends in themselves. Rather than feeling as though she should demonstrate greater commitment and familiarity, which is characteristic of long-time participants, she was satisfied with peripheral involvement. Of course, the fact that she usually did not meet many available men contributed to her transiency.

The tourist role probably is not the most desired nor typical role for older people. However, it does represent a stance that was very attractive to many. They could not socially, politically, or economically afford the instability when they were young. Instead, they found themselves sacrificing their exploratory urges during middle age for the security and social approval found among the stable, well-integrated participants. Of course, it is also important to note that the tourist role has also been forced on many of the aged. They have been removed from positions of stability through retirement, physical disability, loss of a spouse, and other factors. Therefore, the tourist role has not always been voluntary. It is a position that has been self-selected as well as externally imposed.

REGULARS

In this context the term *regular* is used to describe participants who have had much experience with the activities and processes of specific social worlds. They are well-integrated into their spheres of influence and have developed detailed knowledge about what social worlds produce. A primary function of regulars is to provide a measure of stability amidst the constant change found within most worlds. This relatively large body of stable participants tends to be relied upon for many kinds of support. In short, these are the people for whom most activities, events, and processes are organized.

When compared with the two previous stances, regulars stand nearer the core of social world knowledge. While they are not situated at the center of this whirlpool, they are near enough to begin understanding some of the inner workings of those worlds. Collecting, creating, performing, and marketing are the integrating activities most likely to engage regulars. These are ways by which people acquire fairly detailed knowledge of the rules, values, criteria, and evaluatation systems generated by social worlds. However, they do not require knowledge so specialized that only a small number of people could acquire it. Instead, most participants, with enough interest, commitment, and energy, probably could become regulars.

With this in mind, there are four qualities that describe the essence of this stance: (1) an orientation toward the concerns of social worlds best described as *habituation;* (2) the experiences of people with activities and processes that are characterized by relatively deep *integration;* (3) relationships with other participants imbued with a strong sense of *familiarity;* and (4) a commitment to the functioning of worlds best described as *attachment* to their goals, purposes, and plans.

Habituation

As the term implies, *habituation* implies that regulars have structured much of their daily lives around their social worlds. They are the participants found at the conventions, meets, auctions, and exhibits where those in social worlds come together and interact. Similarly, regulars are the ones frequenting the many meeting places, organizing centers, and training centers where they will be recognized by others. In essence, some regulars may be able to lead invisible lives in various social worlds, but most engage in actions that are acknowledged by others. Their linkages, then, probably extend beyond the media into face-to-face meetings with others of the same status and position. The habituation of Arnold and Jean Goodrich (Figure 1.2) in the bowling world illustrates this characteristic. They strictly designated times four days a week for their bowling. These times were rigidly adhered to and given a high priority. The several leagues and groups in which they bowled provided firm commitments that overshadowed all others. Even between seasons, when their leagues were not operating, the Goodrichs bowled on those same days and times. In many ways, their commitment for bowling was the yardstick against which all potential disruptions had to be measured. A crisis with family members or some similar occurrence would, of course, have been allowed to disrupt their schedule. Involvement in this world had become an integral part of their everyday existence. It was something they had done for several years and planned to continue in the future.

Integration

Regulars tend to experience many of the components of social worlds in a wholistic, routinized, and predictable fashion. That is, they tend to know what the components of social worlds are, and how they fit together. Much of this knowledge arises out of their shared biographies with organizational leaders, exemplars, and founding parents of social worlds. Of course, it is not necessary that each and every regular personally know these figures, but they are aware of their contributions through the media. Further, in terms of integration, regulars are bound into social worlds through a vast array of linking devices. Tourists probably have gained access to the most obvious magazines, widely distributed newsletters, and the mass media. Regulars, on the other hand, have access to more esoteric means. They are part of the elaborate networks created and maintained through specialized newsletters, bulletins, journals, personal letters, and telephone calls by which detailed knowledge of social worlds is transmitted.

With regard to geographical spaces, regulars may feel as though they have proprietary rights over access by strangers or tourists. They may, in effect, treat some locations as home territories wherein they are freed from the constraints of the outside world and allowed to pursue their social world activities among equals (Cavan, 1966). For example, regulars in the ballroom dancing world seemed to feel possessive of the community centers, fraternal lodges, and hotel ballrooms where their dances were held. They felt that intrusions by outsiders during the dances were disruptive and disrespectful of their rights. These people had acquired what they believed to be rights to spaces they inhabited only two or three nights a week. The history of their involvement and the importance of the settings in providing integration combined to produce these feelings among the older dancers.

Familiarity

A third quality of this stance is the high degree of *familiarity* regulars have with other participants. They personally know many others like themselves. In fact, the familiarity and long-term relationships that develop may resemble families (Irwin, 1977). That is, through long exposure and repeated contact with others, regulars come to know a great deal about one another. While they probably know most about one another in reference to social world events, activities, and processes, this familiarity will also extend into other portions of the life-round. Regulars may have some awareness of others' family lives, hobbies, problems, and idiosyncracies. For example, older people in the gleaning world had picnics and potlucks to celebrate particularly good hauls of food. At these events, these older people displayed not only their favorite recipes based on the food gathered, but family members as well. It was not uncommon for the children and grandchildren of some gleaners to be paraded out to these events so other regulars might meet, know, and be impressed with them. These events clearly had become family affairs where gleaning provided the impetus for involvement, but only a small portion of total activities. When regulars allow certain social worlds to dominate their lives, it is likely other participants will learn much about their personal lives. For older people, it is this familiarity that may lead to the availability of other kinds of support. That is, networks focused on gleaning were also used by some older people for other kinds of assistance. When rides were needed, or help around the house desired, most had no problems drawing upon relationships formed in that context.

Attachment

The fourth quality of this stance is the fairly high level of personal commitment toward the on-going functioning of social worlds. The term that best characterizes this commitment is *attachment*. It implies an attachment to the ideas and ideologies of those worlds, but it also hints at feelings of belonging among regulars. Fellow participants have become their friends, and involvement in those worlds has become their home. Regulars are participants who continue involvment through thick and thin, good times and bad. In terms of the phases of growth and decline mentioned earlier, regulars will likely continue through the phases of corruption and stagnation when those less committed will drop by the wayside. Involvement, then, may have more relevance for their lives than fads and fashions, although a certain proportion of regulars might also leave during the decline. The presence of regulars is the glue allowing social worlds to coalesce and remain together.

The integrating activities situated older people as regulars were collecting, creating, performing, and marketing. In general, these are the activities that are not easily entered by novices. They require periods of socialization, indoctrination, and personal investment. For the older people interviewed, movement into this role was the end product of many years of stable activity, or a shorter period of very intense involvement. With such an investment, most wanted this role to be stable and to endure.

Just as Erma Martin was the quintessential tourist, Thelma and Thomas Harding embodied the qualities of this stance. As earlier described, the Hardings (Figure 3.4) had maintained a broad range of stable social involvements. Their lives were relatively comfortable, secure, and safe. Over the years they found groups, organizations, associations, and worlds that met their needs and made them feel comfortable. Many of the involvements in the profile were begun in middle age. The family, Masons, and local community activities represented long-standing concerns. They managed to hold on to these activities after retirement and, in effect, substituted several other involvements for those lost. The local senior center and an informal arts and crafts group represented such substitutions. Both involvements required relatively little work on the part of Thomas and Thelma for stable integration. Gleaning, however, demanded much from them and represented the last of the stable involvements they found. They learned the ropes quickly and quickly moved into positions of centrality. Similarly, integration into the gleaning world quickly became an important component of their identities. As the discussion of the final stance will illustrate, the Hardings were well on their way toward the role of insider. Therefore, like most of the older regulars, the Hardings assumed that stance in a world with a sizable proportion of older people involved. The knowledge required for deep integration and the activities necessary to maintain these positions were most easily managed by older people in these worlds. Ballroom dancing with Lucy Anderson and, for a time, Erma Martin represents the other older world with a noticeable number of aged regulars.

INSIDERS

Finally, there remains a small number of participants who stand at the very heart, or core, of social world activities, processes, and events. These *insiders* represent a small elite among the masses of others within social worlds. Insiders have a great deal of experience with the processes of social worlds and know the intimate details of their organization, orientation, and stock of knowledge. Clearly, these are the organizational leaders, opinion leaders, exemplars, and founding parents mentioned in an earlier chapter. As the inner circle of social world participants, insiders must assure others of a smoothly operating, fully functioning, and viable social world.

When compared with regulars, those who are insiders have much more control over information, knowledge, and activities within social worlds. They are, in effect, located at the center of the whirlpool of social knowledge existing within worlds. Insiders constitute an extremely small proportion of all participants and, in many ways, control the actions and activities of others. In addition, while movement into this role might be a logical step for regulars, the path is strewn with roadblocks. That is, transition very much depends upon the personal acceptability, skills, and fortitude of the people involved. Becoming an insider is not automatic with the expenditure of much time, energy, and resources. Potential insiders must demonstrate their commitment and knowledge over long periods of time and in the presence of the right people. Social world insiders, in order to cope with the demands of the role, may scale down involvement in other activities. They simply do not have the time nor resources to be deeply integrated in concerns other than their social world and, perhaps, the family.

There were three integrating activities that propelled one older person into the role of insider. Through organizing, representing, and evaluating, Henry Farley (Figure 3.3.) was the only one who approached this level of integration. All three activities imply the strategic use of knowledge and resources unavailable to strangers, tourists, and regulars. With this in mind, the following four qualities describe the essence of this type: (1) the orientation toward the concerns of specific social worlds is so pervasive that it comprises the total *identity* of the person; (2) experiences within these social worlds are focused toward the *creation* of experiences for those less deeply integrated; (3) there is a strong tendency for *intimate* relationships to develop with other participants; and (4) the *recruitment* of new members and the continuing integration of existing participants is a primary commitment of people adopting this stance.

Identity

For the most part, the existence and perceptions of insiders revolve around specific social worlds. The investment in time, energy, and resources by the people involved would require a decrease in other activities and involvements. For example, Henry Farley began to devote much less time to the Kiwanis, Rotary, and Chamber of Commerce organizations as he became more deeply integrated into gleaning. As his profile illustrates, he had very few important social involvements beyond gleaning and the family. For older people like Henry Farley, the identity of social world insider may be carried over into other settings and situations. When Henry attended meetings at senior centers, fraternal orders, and civic organizations, he was there as a gleaner, not as a member of the other groups. The identity created in gleaning had become so important for his sense of self and well-being that it was invoked in most social situations. He was, in effect, Henry Farley the gleaner above and beyond all else.

Creation

While tourists and regulars tend to seek only familiarity and acceptance within social worlds, insiders are those who control, direct, and create experiences for other participants. The integrating activities situating people in this role are evidence of this tendency. Through organizing, representing, and evaluating, insiders find themselves in positions where large numbers of other participants depend upon them for guidance or direction. As organizer and representative for the gleaners, Henry Farley found himself at many community meetings, legislative hearings, and senior center gatherings for the purposes of creating ties with food producers, community leaders, and larger numbers of older people. He described this aspect of his position in an interview from which the following excerpt was taken.

> I often have to spend a lot of time just traveling around the area talking about what we, the gleaners, are all about. When I say area, I mean Sacramento, surrounding towns, and even sometimes in the Bay Area. I guess the most important reason for all this talking and traveling around is to make contacts. You know, we really depend upon the good graces and thoughtfulness of a lot of people. Farmers, growers, agribusiness concerns, food banks, and manufacturers are just a few of the resources we have taken from in the last, say, couple of years. The whole thing, I mean gleaning, really depends upon how well we are able to put together this network of contacts who will contact us first if there is food to be picked up. I just recently heard about an apricot rancher up near Chico who won't be able to sell his crop because of the size and quality of his fruit. We need to contact him in the next day or so, just to make sure he doesn't let it all go to waste. . . .

In effect, Henry had to spend vast amounts of time on organizational work so the vast network of older people, growers, and producers could be brought into play. If crops to be wasted or packaged food to be thrown away could not be located, the gleaners were without a function.

Intimacy

The relationships of insiders with others in social worlds are best described by the term *intimacy*. In this context, the term has three general meanings. First, it implies that insiders tend to develop warm and close personal relationships with other participants. The sheer length of time devoted to such activities, coupled with the shared commitments of all concerned, would lead to the development of lasting friendships among those involved. Second, the term intimacy also describes the access of insiders to facts, figures, and data largely unavailable to others. Access to the intimate knowledge about the nature of activities within gives insiders knowledge about other participants that otherwise would be concealed. For example, insiders probably stand at the intersection of more networks than do those less deeply integrated. Consequently, they have access to more sources of information relevant to the functioning of specific social worlds. Third, insiders tend to be highly visible personages to regulars, tourists, and strangers. They may be prominent figures at conventions, auctions, meets, and exhibits at which their names and faces become widely known. As a result, large numbers of participants may feel as though they are, at least, superficially acquainted with insiders. By seeing the their faces at events over the years, a certain kind of situational intimacy may develop. For examples many older gleaners who had never met Henry Farley knew of his reputation and personality. They occasionally referred to him by first name, even though he probably had no idea who they were, or of their status in the gleaners.

Recruitment

Finally, insiders tend to be so highly committed to their social worlds that the *recruitment* of new participants becomes a central concern. Through their years of involvement, people who have adopted this stance probably have seen many strangers, tourists, and regulars move through their domain. Therefore, in order to protect their personal investment, insiders must engage in actions to ensure the existence of their social worlds. Since people do not enter social worlds through territorial relocation or ascribed traits, active recruitment is necessary. The quote by Henry Farley regarding the creating of gleaning activities also implied the importance of recruitment. Finding new members was a secondary goal of Henry's as he went from group to group spreading the word about the gleaners. Clearly, those typed as regulars might also engage in recruitment, but no group of participants recognizes the importance of this process more than insiders.

The profiles of strangers, tourists, regulars, and insiders encapsulate the experiences of people located at various points within social worlds. Through these types, then, a better understanding of the kinds and degrees of knowledge, perception, and involvement that stratify people integrated into social worlds might be achieved. Especially for the aged, these profiles may serve as the foundation for a processual analysis of social integration. The lives of the major characters in this study were testimony to the fact that older people do not necessarily lose touch with social life, and move into positions of less centrality than they had during middle age. Instead, their lives illustrate the kinds of changes and sacrifices that had to take place if they were going to achieve satisfactory integration. For some, satisfactory integration meant stable involvement in a broad range of activities, while several others jettisoned peripheral activities to focus on specific social worlds. Most important, a sizeable number of other older people seemed to use old age as a time free of heavy responsibilities. The tourist role typifies their approach to social world involvement and social life in general.

This set of social types sets the stage for analysis of movement through social worlds by the major characters of this study. Social integration is a process and the social types represent analytic points with the whirlpools of knowledge, activities, and processes in social worlds. Therefore, by using the four stances, changes in integration of the older people will be traced, with factors encouraging or discouraging integration documented. In this way, routes and avenues of integration will be identified, as well as movement of some older people out of social worlds. Differences in the routes traveled by the aged had implications for the evaluation of their lives by friends, relatives, and social service personnel.

NOTES

1. This chapter is a revised and expanded version of an earlier paper (Unruh, 1979). The relevance of these social types in several contexts is further discussed in two other pieces. The first, Unruh (1980a), summarizes the use of the social types for understanding the situation of older people, while the second, Unruh (1980b), briefly mentions them in the formal analysis of social worlds per se.

2. The study of regulars in a variety of social organizational forms has been the focus of many urban ethnographies and community studies. Regulars were the nucleus around which William F. Whyte's *Streetcorner Society* (1955), Elliot Liebow's *Tally's Corner* (1967), and Herbert Gans's *Urban Villagers* (1962) revolved. Through many studies, it has been possible to follow some activities in the worlds of art, fashion, sports, convicts, and various professions (Becker, 1976; Goode, 1957; Irwin, 1970b; Karp et al., 1977).

6

INTEGRATION AS SOCIAL PROCESS

The set of four social types identifies some important differences among people in social worlds. The stances of stranger, tourist, regular, and insider represent different locations of people with regard to the knowledge, activities, events, and processes generated within social worlds. Using these stances as a foundation, this chapter focuses on the ways older people changed their roles, stances, and positions within various social worlds. Along the way, a number of routes along which the aged traveled will be discussed so their movement among the four stances may be plotted. In this way, important changes in identity and perspective will be documented and integration as a social process will be analyzed.

Throughout this chapter special attention will be given to differences between personal conceptions of integration among older people and those of friends, families, relatives, and social service personnel. This is interesting and important because many studies of personal change among the aged have adopted a vantage point far above the nitty gritty of their daily lives (see Atchley, 1980; Babchuk and Booth, 1969; Cumming and Henry, 1961; Gordon et al., 1976; Rosow, 1967, 1974). Emphasis on experiential changes among specific older people will expose the internal logic of some changes in integration that followed courses and had personal meanings for the aged that were not understood by those around them. While some of the aged viewed changes in integration as logical and reasonable moves, many people around them believed they must be detrimental to their well-being. Of course, some changes are negative and detrimental to the lives of the aged, but such is not necessarily the case (see Bultena and Wood, 1969; Lowenthal and Robinson, 1976; Streib and Streib, 1975; Taietz and Larson, 1956). The analysis of integration as social process begins by focusing on what will be termed conventional changes.

CONVENTIONAL CHANGES

In everyday life people tend to develop ideas about how new identities and perspectives are achieved. Similarly, sociologists who have studied these changes have developed benchmarks and models that render these processes understandable. For example, sociological studies of religious conversion (Lofland and Stark, 1965; Lofland, 1977), illnesses (Davis, 1963; Roth, 1963), medical training (Hall, 1948), and the transition to parenthood (Rossi, 1968) all have made use of stages, steps, or phases to capture the essence of the changes. The stances of stranger, tourist, regular, and insider are no different. They have been intended to isolate essential kinds of changes out of the array of activities and confusions of everyday life. The imagery of change implied by these stances is that of people moving more deeply into the structure of social worlds which have stratified layers of relevance (Schutz, 1962, 1970).

In essence, the arrangement of the four stances suggests a kind of common sense logic about social integration. This logic implies that people usually begin in the role of stranger and become tourists, regulars, and insiders in that order. Clearly, not all social world participants will become insiders, or even regulars, but the common sense logic implies that they move in that direction. This often is the expected course of integration, and progress is defined in this way. Therefore, based upon conceptions of integration in everyday life, the term *conventional changes* will be used in reference to transformations of identity and perspective that followed this course.[1]

| | Social Types | | | |
	Strangers	*Tourists*	*Regulars*	*Insiders*
Orientation	Naivete	Curiosity	Habituation	Identity
Experiences	Disorientation	Learning	Integration	Creation
Relationships	Superficiality	Transiency	Familiarity	Intimacy
Commitment	Detachment	Entertainment	Attachment	Recruitment

Figure 6.1: Types of Social World Integration

Figure 6.1 summarizes the model presented in the previous chapter and portrays logical changes in orientation, experience, relationships, and commitment of people in social worlds. In analyzing the experiences of the major characters of this study, it is necessary to look at the older people who tended to follow this course in various social worlds. Therefore, the *conventional process* is the first, and perhaps primary, route by which the aged changed their perspectives and identities.

The Conventional Process

Of course, strangers exist at the outer regions of the whirlpool of social world knowledge. They generally do not understand nor care about the shared interests and perspectives uniting others. Lucy Anderson's failure to understand the meaning ascribed to Avon bottles and other items important to her friend marked her as an outsider, or disinterested observer. Movement from the stance of stranger to tourist must include the suspension of distrust, suspicion, and perceptions of meaninglessness in favor of curiosity about the activities of various social worlds. In effect, people move into the tourist role when social worlds become accessible, when a potential for personal relevance is identified, and when they feel a certain degree of receptivity from others. The combination of these factors may then stimulate an increased desire for people to expend the energy necessary for learning the unique roles, rules, values, vocabularies, perceptions, and experiences of social worlds.[2]

When compared with other age groups, the problems encountered by the aged in making the transition from stranger to tourist were great. First, some of them were removed from the networks of communication that might have informed them of the potential relevance and receptivity of a broad range of social worlds. For example, there seemed to be a tendency among the predominantly middle-aged people who organized senior centers, retirement communities, and housing complexes to expose the aged to activities in which the aged were presumed to be interested. More than a few of the older people interviewed were dismayed at the response of these organizers to their suggestions. While some older people sought new or unusual experiences, their efforts largely were vetoed by the middle-aged people in power. One of the older women offered several examples of suggested activities, events, programs, and trips that did not materialize. The following excerpt illustrates one instance.

> At one time, many of us got together and decided we would like to have someone from the Bay Area come to teach transcendental meditation, yoga, and other Eastern ideas. Well, I mean to tell you, the woman at the senior center in charge of these sorts of things didn't like the idea at all. She thought it would be foolish to have "a bunch of old people doing things like that." This is just one example of many. Some of the people running the place down there have very elitist attitudes . . . and seem to know better than we do what we want. . . . A bunch of us ladies were talking and, you know, if you're stifled like that so many times, well you just stop trying to suggest new ideas and activities.

With regard to social world integration, experiences like those at this senior center discouraged older people from seeking new involvements by embarrassing, humiliating, and placing obstacles in the paths of those who might continue seeking. For example, the older person who was still interested in Eastern meditation had to discover the places, linking devices, and networks of communication on his or her own. On the other hand, if the activities had been there to sample, some might have participated in them and had the choice of accepting, ignoring, or rejecting their potential relevance.

A second problem encountered by the aged relates to the introduction of new ideas and activities at places where older people congregate — namely, senior centers, retirement communities, and nursing homes. Organizers of these places have included activities designed to encourage further integration into various social worlds. A local senior center, for example, conducted classes in watercolor techniques, beginning photography, needlepoint, and art appreciation. While these activities seemed to fill the hours of elderly participants, few of them ever pursued these involvements beyond the center. Most seemed content to engage in these activities with those their own age in familiar surroundings. At one point in the interview, Robert Peterson (Figure 2.3) offered some insight into the matter. He noted that the local senior center was one of the first places they visited after moving to Northern California from Arizona. He and

Sarah had heard that there were some older people interested in art who regularly met there. What they found, as Robert described, were art activities far removed from those deemed legitimate in the art world.

> Well, my wife and I went over there once when we first moved to town. . . . We had heard they occasionally had art activities there, and we want to see what was going on. As a result of our visit, we are not very keen on having to resort to that sort of thing to keep up our interest in living. Actually, I find that sort of thing depressing. . . . What we saw were a bunch of people sitting around going through magazines and cutting out pictures for collages and that sort of thing. I think a person can maintain their interest in life if they don't learn how to paste things in scrapbooks, do handiwork, or even play scrabble . . . all that just for the sake of killing time.

To someone like Robert Peterson, deeply integrated into the art world, the activities he found were both watered-down and inauthentic. To him, they did nothing to teach the older people there about art, its definition, guidelines for understanding, or criteria for evaluating. In this instance older people were being taught skills and knowledge that might, at best, keep them in the tourist role. To some degree the kinds of things these people were learning were so far removed from the legitimate concerns of the art world that they did not enter that domain at all. Consequently, they remained involved at the senior center and were not lost to the larger world of art.

People moving into the tourist role, then, must have gained a curiosity about specific social worlds based on legitimate information. They continue to seek experiences that might be instructive about what life is like as a bonafide members of the art, music, stamp, bicycling, or automobile collecting worlds. As Robert Peterson implied, one factor that might lead people into the role of tourist is knowledge about the differences between authentic and inauthentic products, ideas, activities, or experiences.

As earlier noted, the stance of tourist is marked by a degree of transiency with little long-term commitment. As the quintessential tourist, Erma Martin's (Figure 2.4) experiences may shed some light on movement into that role. With regard to the world of bowling, Erma entered with every intention of becoming a regular. She believed bowling would be fun and interesting, and would facilitate the formation of new friends. However, despite her curiosity, Erma lost interest after repeated exposure to the activities and events characterizing that world. In effect, the world did not turn out to be the way it seemed, nor were the people, activities, events, and interpersonal connections the kind she sought. In her words,

> I bowled for a while and belonged to a team last year. It was really more than a bowling league. . . . We would occasionally get together for other things as a group, and we became pretty well acquainted. This was not a senior citizen's league, but one that included a lot of different people. The bowling group kept my attention for some time. I guess all of a sudden, I just started getting to the point where I just wasn't interested. The more I lost interest the worse it got. . . . You know, bowling itself is okay for a few months, but after a while, these people began to take it so seriously. I think there was a lot of pressure to have a good game every time. I just wasn't interested in the pressure after a few months. . . .

In effect, Erma's curiosity about bowling was satisfied before she had become well-integrated into that world and developed long-standing commitments. Clearly, she was not willing to stick with it through good times and bad. Since involvement in the bowling world turned out to be more serious and less sociable than Erma imagined, she eventually lost interest, failed to build commitment, and faded from the scene. It is interesting to note that Erma, perhaps because of the degree to which she was a tourist in many activities, felt no sense of loss or remorse for not fitting into the bowling world. Instead, she accepted it as a risk people have to take if they are daring enough to try new and different things.

Among the older people interviewed, movement from the role of tourist to that of regular occurred in a number of ways. Some eventually became regulars after long periods of involvement. Through trial and error they learned the rules and managed to work their way in. Such was the case with older people in the worlds of bicycling, art, and dancing. However, in rare instances there were older people who moved through the roles of stranger and tourist in very little time. The experiences of Thelma and Thomas Harding (Figure 3.4) illustrate the rapid rate at which these changes have occurred. In the following interview excerpt, Thelma describes the very short period between their introduction to the gleaning world and their relatively deep integration into its concerns.

> We were down at the senior center one day. We were there for the senior meal with some old friends. Well, Henry Farley came there and gave the first talk on gleaning he had done in our city. We were all very impressed and very interested. So we were going to be on vacation when he set the time for the first meeting in this city, so Bill and Rita went and joined right away. We came back in time for the second meeting and joined up. So we've been involved since almost the beginning of such activity in this area. When they started the meetings, Henry would say, "Now, all right, who would like to do this?" and "Who would like to do that?" Well, I ended up saying that I would help telephone. . . . I ended up being chief of telephone operators for the telephone tree. Now, we use just about our whole house for things related to gleaning. . . . Actually, I guess, all of these things happened within a time of just a few weeks, maybe a month. . . .

This brief narrative highlights the rapid movement of Thelma and Thomas into the roles of regular in the gleaning world. First, they came into contact with that social world during the very early phase of expansion. Henry Farley had contacted other older people in Northern California communities and sought to create a network of available volunteers. In effect, the system of activities, processes, events, and activities, which eventually constituted gleaning, were just being created when the Hardings became interested. They became members of the core circle, therefore, quite easily and fairly rapidly. There did not seem to be a cadre of long-time participants who already occupied positions of responsibility. If there had been, Thelma and Thomas might have had to wait for new leadership positions to open up. Instead, they were available at the time Henry Farley conceived of the roles and positions. Second, they rather quickly became core members of the gleaners because of the close match between the ideology of gleaning and their existing interests. Thelma continually emphasized the fact they had been thrifty their entire married lives. They scrimped and saved for nearly everything they bought, and believed that nothing should be wasted. This same attitude formed the basis for Henry Farley's notion of gleaning from the very beginning. Consequently, Thelma and Thomas did not have to spend a good deal of time floundering about trying to discover the ideology. Instead, they knew it and had incorporated it into their lives for many years. Similarly, little time probably was spent by older people already in the gleaners trying to decide whether the Hardings had the commitment, physical capabilities, and charitable impulses necessary. Older people in social worlds where an obvious match between their existing interests and those required of established participants may have to endure a long period of apprenticeship. At that time, they must prove that they have gained sufficient knowledge and commitment to warrant the status of regular participant. In youthful and age-mixed worlds, older people have had the problem of having their involvement viewed as cute, marginal, or frivolous. Some younger participants seemed unwilling to take older people seriously and, consequently, made the transition from tourist to regular more difficult. For example, if there was a job to be done or a role to be filled, these people immediately thought of younger participants. The implication being that older people were not thought competent or, perhaps, worthy of investing a great deal of effort into since they probably did not have many years of involvement left. Therefore, the third reason why the Hardings moved so easily into the role of regular was that there was no group of insiders seeking to cool out, prohibit, or otherwise impede the careers of some tourists. Through the control of linking devices, organizing centers, meeting places, clearing houses, and other esoteric materials, insiders potentially have control over the kinds of people who acquire intimate knowledge of their social worlds. Far more control is exerted over those who aspire to become insiders than those who wish to adopt the stances of regular or tourist.

In most social worlds it is apparent the aged constitute an undeveloped and overlooked resource (Atchley, 1976; Binstock, 1972, 1974; Butler 1969, 1975; Lopata, 1970; Rose, 1965; Shanas, 1970). For the most part, the strategies and actions of insiders designed to recruit new participants generally ignore the availability of huge numbers of willing, able, and eager older people. The kinds of media employed to publicize the activities and events of various social worlds largely excluded those dominated by the aged. For example, if insiders in the bicycling world had publicized their races and events, a larger number of older people might have been drawn in the role of spectator. Many races were held within walking distance of the local senior center and central business district around which many of the aged lived. This would have been the first step toward drawing some of them more deeply into that world. Similarly, in the case of radio and television advertising, the time of day and program used for publicity says much about the kind of participants sought. Public service spots are available in both radio and television. If they were employed strategically, it is possible older people might be informed of social world events with which they might have been unfamiliar. Further, consider the content of editorials and advertising in magazines devoted to photography, gourmet cooking, science, sports, art, and so on. Rarely are older people portrayed as active and vital participants in these worlds (Francher, 1973; Hess, 1974). Instead, when older people are sought, it generally is through various old age associations or senior centers. These are places where, for the most part, only certain kinds of older people might come into contact with the information.

Encouraging Conventional Changes

With this in mind, it is necessary to give some explicit attention to ways conventional changes are facilitated. To better explore this matter, the discussion will be organized around three factors that emerged in the interviews. These facilitants seemed to arise for older people after they had found the concerns of particular worlds personally relevant, interactionally accessible, and receptive. In short, the following three facilitants represent the combined efforts of both older people seeking deeper integration, and established social world participants working to aid them in their quests. *Creating roles, incurring obligations,* and *investing resources* are the three predominant facilitants to be discussed. To those familiar with commitment building processes found in other contexts, the three facilitants should strike a familiar note. They closely resemble those found in studies of integration into other social organizational forms (Arnold, 1970; Becker, 1960; Becker et al., 1961; Blau, 1974; Hausknecht, 1962; Kanter, 1972; Lofland, 1977; Lofland and Stark, 1965; and Poplin, 1979). Therefore, it is important to keep in mind the relevance of these factors for the integration of older people into social worlds.

Creating roles. One of the best ways to build commitment toward a group, association, organization, or community is to give people offices to hold, positions to fill, or jobs to do. By *creating roles* for other participants, leaders communicate that recipients are acceptable for continued involvement, worthy of greater responsibility, and possess traits important for representing the larger group.

In reference to older people in social worlds, insiders' use of this strategy had three important effects. First, this strategy more deeply situated older people into the communication networks that bind worlds together. By assuming official positions in social worlds, the aged were placed near a node in the webs of communication, interaction, and information dispersal so critical to the continuation of social worlds. For example, Thelma Harding's early decision (and opportunity) to organize the telephone tree, by which information of activities was dispersed to participants, quickly situated her at a node of both information reception and dispersal. She rapidly had become a person with primary responsibility for informing vital participants of gleaner-related news. Second, this action similarly drew older people closer to the systems of meeting places, organizing centers, training centers, and other spaces where people met. These positions of high visibility made the few older people involved more likely to meet others face-to-face with similar interests. Therefore, relationships based on shared interests often resulted. Eventually, some turned into long-standing liaisons reaching into all corners of their lives. Third, personal access to knowledge about events, activities, and processes was enhanced through the adoption of roles. This led to increased control over the actions of others less deeply integrated. Consequently, the cognitive ties with insiders were felt more strongly, while the ties with those on the periphery were less intense. For example, over time the Hardings came to feel much closer to Henry Farley than the occasional university student who would participate irregularly in gleaning activities. Because they knew how much Farley and the gleaners depended upon the willingness of a stable core of people to drop everything if a food pick-up was called, the Hardings felt even more obliged to be part of that group.

Use of this strategy by social world insiders tended to draw targeted participants away from consuming, collecting, creating, and performing, which tend to be undertaken in solo. As a result some older people were drawn toward the acts of marketing, organizing, representing, and evaluating, which brought them into face-to-face contact with other participants. For the aged, this strategy meant they were drawn away from isolated and solitary modes of social world involvement where use of the media was the dominant linkage with others. They were, in effect, simultaneously drawn into the company of others and more deeply into the structure of various social worlds (Christ, 1965; Hochschild, 1973, 1978; Jacobs, 1974; Rose, 1965). Such certainly was the case with Robert and Sarah Peterson when they moved to the Phoenix area. Through their friends at the local art museum, they quickly acquired the roles of security guard, board member, and committee chair. In these ways, the Petersons found both purpose and position in one corner of the art world.

Incurring obligations. Of course the adoption of specific social world roles carries with it a number of obligations. Through the process of *incurring obligations* these older people were not only required to carry on a shared present as they conducted their everyday lives, but to project a shared future as well. Once these roles were assumed, there were jobs to do, people to contact, activities to organize, products to evaluate, and so on. These obligations required the older people to structure and organize their time so that all projects could be completed. A major portion of that process was the matter of projecting into the future the course of their participation. For example, Thelma and Thomas Harding, in a sense obliged themselves to continued involvement in gleaning by assuming central roles. They believed that the smooth and orderly operation of gleaning depended upon use of their front porch for distribution of foodstuffs, Thelma's organization of the telephone tree, and their active involvement in picking up items. While gleaning probably would have continued as an enterprise whether or not the Hardings were so actively involved, it was their belief that it would not that proved important. That belief bound them into the system of shared perspectives and understandings more effectively than any amount of coercion. Another kind of felt obligation bound Fred Romano into the bicycling world at a time when he might have just as easily withdrawn. Much of Fred's identity and reputation was based on his bicycling. Therefore, continued involvement in the bicycling world was not only a matter of preserving his personal identity, but also that of saving and extending his reputation among people whose opinions he valued.

Stable participation was not a problem until the accident when his leg was broken. It earlier was noted that Fred had great difficulty mustering the stamina, desire, and strength to work his way back on a bicycle, into condition, and back to competition. In this context it is most important to note the obligations which, in effect, forced him to work hard on the recovery process. During the interview he recalled the continual encouragement and cajoling of his wife, which convinced him that he was as important to bicycling as it was to him. In his words, Alice Romano's continual encouragement and reminders of what people expected of him was a major factor.

> Well, you know, when I was stuck here in the house waiting for my leg to heal, I got really depressed. These things take so long. . . . Here I was hobbling around for months. One thing that really seemed to help was Alice. She would always talk about how excited I used to be back when I was riding. Oh, and another thing. She would talk about some of our bicycling friends and tell me about how much people were waiting for me to get back into it. You know, it got to the point where I had to get back into shape and show them what was left in this old man. . . .

In a sense, Fred had incurred the felt obligation to continue bicycling not only for himself and his friends, but for old people everywhere. He came to view himself as a symbol of what the aged are capable of doing if they have the courage, stamina, and resources necessary for this kind of activity. Therefore, he seemed to feel that the options available to him were limited. If he allowed a broken leg to remove him from active involvement, it would have caused irreparable damage to the persona he built over the years. On the other hand, the hard work and dedication necessary to strengthen his legs and work his way back into competition would only strengthen and solidify an identity of great personal importance (see Unruh, 1983).

This process closely relates to Howard S. Becker's (1960) discussion of "side bets." In everyday life, people tend to evolve interests in certain activities that originally had nothing to do with the task, activity, or involvement at hand. For example, Fred Romano rather quickly acquired the personal identity of bicyclist and built a national reputation around it. It was not something he strategically planned when he began, but it developed nonetheless. As a result, the number of options available to him following the accident were severely limited. In his case, the making of a side bet revolving around an identity that became important to him tended to situate him even more deeply into the bicycling world. Similarly, during the 1960s and 1970s, Robert and Sarah Peterson felt the obligation to continue active involvement in the social world of internees. At the time, they truly believed that world would disintegrate without their help. Eventually, their participation decreased in both frequency and intensity, but it was a felt obligation which kept them involved until they were in their mid-80s.

Investing resources. This factor is related to that of incurring obligations. The resources many older people invested in various social worlds were social, personal, and economic. In this context, the discussion of *investing resources* will be restricted to economic and material investments of the aged. Especially for older people, the matter of economic investments in various activities may be of great personal concern (Munnell, 1977; Schulz, 1980). Most important, these investments often constrained the options of some older people in various social worlds. For example, in addition to his social and psychological investment in bicycling, Fred Romano also had considerable economic resources tied up in the activity. Therefore, if he had allowed the accident to remove him from bicycling, he would have lost an important identity, a good measure of positive self-concept, and thousands of dollars invested in bicycling equipment. Similarly, one older female artist had a considerable investment in art books, paints, canvases, and sculpting materials even though she lived on a meager income. Perhaps largely in an implicit and vague way, economic investments served as an incentive for both of these older people to remain deeply involved in their respective activities. By the same token, it is also important to note those people who have invested in expensive cameras, antique automobiles, paintings, golf clubs, and course of instruction in the hope that these investments would force them to become more deeply integrated into various social worlds. Clearly, the acquisition of expensive objects or materials has not located people very deeply into social worlds. However, the feeling that such actions become incentives for greater personal, intellectual, and social involvement was not uncommon.

Evaluating Conventional Changes

To this point, this chapter has focused on older people who tended to follow a conventional route of change within various social worlds. That is, they tended to move through the stances of stranger, tourist, regular, and insider in that order. Clearly, not every older person mentioned moved so deeply into the structure of their social world that the terms regular or insider applied. However, their movements conformed to the imagery of people achieving greater increments of experience and knowledge as they were propelled into the activities, processes, and events of various social worlds.

In everyday life, many people feel that this progression represents the most desirable, satisfactory, and personally rewarding route of personal change. As a result, the changes in involvement experienced by older people generally were judged and evaluated according to this model. The societal attitude underlying this model of change arose in conversation at many points. In speaking about the experiences of friends, for example, some people would express the belief that those who failed to move beyond the roles of stranger or tourist did so because they lacked the necessary dedication and fortitude. The work ethic imagery was applied by some to all areas of personal and social life. The following interview excerpt illustrates this point. The speaker is an older woman who had been involved in various worlds of dance for a long time. On that basis, she offered some suggestions regarding the ways older people should pursue their social activities and involvements.

> Keep busy and you'll get there. . . . I don't know what I would do if not for the senior center. I guess I'd be home a lot since most of the dances I go to are held there. Live while you can, if there is something you like to do, or are interested in, pursue it and stick with it. I have been involved down here for many years and seen people come and go. You know, some of these people just don't really give the dances a chance. They will start coming to dances but then let just about any little thing keep them from coming out again.

In a similar vein, another older woman offered her observations on the commitment of most seniors involvement at the local senior center. At the age of 74, the speaker had become a coordinator of travel at the senior center and, consequently, rose to a prominent position. Even though her observation was directed toward those she came across in her work at the senior center, it has broader relevance.

> Many seniors in this city should learn how to participate, not just buy membership cards. They have so many resources they have never tapped in their own personal lives and at the center that they have no need to feel neglected by their children or their friends. Older people should broaden their horizons by becoming involved with their peers. . . . If they would just give it a try and stick with it for awhile, they could do themselves some good. . . .

Interestingly, many who successfully have completed the process of conventional change believed that those who had not were short-changed, uncommitted, lazy, or even failures. In essence, the belief was that if older people were not integrated into society it was due to some personal deficiency or failure. In a similar vein, some who study the lives of the aged would believe that those who drop out, remain marginally involved, or are not visibly engaged in various corners of social life necessarily are disengaged or lonely (Atchley, 1980; Bild and Havighurst, 1976; Hanssen et al., 1978). However, based upon the experiences of some older people in various social worlds, some other possibilities and alternative explanations begin to loom larger. It is possible that at least some of the aged perceived by others to be disengaged, marginal, and lonely may have followed routes of personal change not understood by outsiders.

UNCONVENTIONAL CHANGES

Throughout this study it has been noted that personal involvement in social worlds is characterized by a high degree of informality. People may identify with various social worlds and move in and out of their domains with relative ease. In short, explicit awareness or acknowledgment by others is not necessary for meaningful integration. Largely for this reason, changes in personal involvement by the aged that did not follow the conventional route tended to be misunderstood and misperceived. The highly informal character of social world involvement made the knowledge that outsiders had about the careers of certain older people incomplete.

In this context, then, *unconventional changes* are those that did not follow the set of four stances as earlier described. That is, they were personal changes not accurately captured nor explained in terms of the stranger, tourist, regular, and insider progression. However, these stances remain useful as points of reference regarding location within the structures of social worlds. In this way some routes of change will be identified that had a degree of internal logic, rationality, and sensibility not easily understood by people other than the aged who were involved. Integration as social process will be analyzed from a different vantage point.

Routes of Unconventional Change

In this section five routes of unconventional change will be identified and discussed. They represent courses of integration followed by some older people in social worlds that ran counter to the logic of most observers. Therefore, whenever possible the evaluation of these routes by friends and acquaintances of the older people involved will be noted. The routes to be analyzed are: (1) *shortcircuiting,* (2) *backtracking,* (3) *stalemating,* (4) *rebounding,* and (5) *bailing out.*

Shortcircuiting. On occasion, there have been people who entered the domains of various social worlds and rapidly moved into the roles of regular and insider. When several of the conventional stances were bypassed in a very short period of time, the route of integration might be termed *shortcircuiting.* Crucial to this route is the widespread belief among other participants that those who have shortcircuited the conventional route have moved too quickly and, thereby, shortchanged either the group or themselves. By moving too quickly, some insiders have speculated that people did not properly learn the standards and procedures of the social worlds into which they were integrated. In effect, those engaged in shortcircuiting were perceived as not paying their dues by experiencing the trials and tribulations that beset typical participants. At worst, there may be a perception that those engaged in this process have been insincere, self-serving, or are somehow betraying the best interests of social worlds.

Few changes among the older people interviewed could be seen as examples of this route. One of the older people interviewed reported how a retired businessman moved into the community and sought to take control of many activities among the square dancers. Evidently, a certain amount of resentment built up among long-time dancers who sought to put him in his place. The very rapid integration of Thelma and Thomas Harding into the gleaning world might have been considered to be an example of shortcircuiting. They very quickly moved from the role of stranger to that of regular. However, their rapid integration did not create resentment among other participants because of the expansion of the gleaning world. They were not viewed as taking jobs, roles, and prestige away from other, more deserving participants. Instead, they simply were filling a vacuum near the center of activities. However, had the Hardings become involved several years later, when gleaning was more established, they might have angered other gleaners with their rapid integration.

Backtracking. More frequently, older people worked their way into various social worlds via the conventional route only to realize they preferred a lesser role. The stances of insider and regular tend to carry with them many obligations and commitments. For some, the pressures and demands of relatively deep integration in various social worlds proved to be burdensome. Therefore, some engaged in *backtracking,* which served to locate them in preferred positions. A number of reasons arose that may account for the backward movement of certain older people in social worlds. For the most part, the reasons were discussed as age-related influences in an earlier chapter. In this context it is most important to note the social effects of these changes rather than the role of disabilities, scarce economic resources, residential relocation, and family status on social integration.

This process is implied in the work of Chad Gordon and associates (1976), which documents changes in leisure activities and intensity of involvement across the life cycle. Of the major characters in this study, the movement of Robert and Sarah Peterson in the world of internees best illustrates this route. At one point in their lives, it was noted that they believed it necessary to act as insiders if that world were to survive. With advancing age, the effort proved too demanding. Therefore, they withdrew from the activities of organizing events and maintaining communication among participants, and settled back into a lesser role. Consequently, they no longer were overwhelmed by the activity and continued to participate in events organized by others. In a sense, the Peterson's use of this route might be said to resemble the process of social disengagement. In fact, their daughter believed her parents to be approaching total disengagement. While they used to attend reunions of the internees as a family, she believed she soon would become the only representative. From the perspective of Robert and Sarah themselves, they believed that backtracking had allowed them to hold onto that world at a time when they were not engaged in much else. Rather than proceeding toward complete disengagement, they believed they could stay in touch with the few peers they had left for several more years. Two interpretations of their move arise when comparing their perceptions with those of their daughter. The daughter saw it was the beginning of the end of social involvement, while they perceived it as a way of holding on, rather than letting go. A vital component of this unconventional route, then, is the willingness to recede back to former roles while continuing to share the perspectives and interests of that world.

Stalemating. Conventional change implies increasing movement toward the core of social world knowledge. The assumption being that increments in knowledge and position should bring people more deeply into the structure of various social worlds. Clearly, many of the major characters in this study never achieved central positions. The route of *stalemating,* then, refers to the special circumstances under which these people became locked or frozen into certain positions. These were people who seemed to possess the talents, skills, and attributes necessary for deep integration, but somehow remained in what others around them defined as inferior roles. This is the circumstance the term stalemating seeks to describe.

Friends and acquaintances of one older woman believed she should have been more deeply integrated into the art world than she had been. Her situation has been mentioned in other contexts, but it is enough here to note that she was partially disabled as a result of an automobile accident. Partially paralyzed, she engaged in painting and sculpting for both personal fulfillment and therapy. To those who knew her, this artist seemed stuck somewhere between the roles of tourist and regular. She seemed competent enough to them so that she could have become a local figure, but somewhat hesitant to make the move. To facilitate further integration, some friends and family members encouraged her to participate in local art events to a greater degree than she had in the past. When viewed from the disabled artist's perspective, the stalemating seemed to result from a logical and rational decision not to pursue greater involvement. She believed that more time devoted to painting and displaying her art would have detracted from organizing activities in the housing unit where she lived. Largely because of her disability, she simply did not have the energy necessary to achieve and maintain deep integration in several forms of social organization. She had been given a partial subsidy by the managers of her housing complex for the expressed purpose of organizing the older residents there into a relatively cohesive body. While she did not feel especially successful in the task, it was a priority that forced her to remain stalemated in the art world.

Rebounding. When people involved in a particular social world withdraw for a noticeable period of time and then resume involvement, they have followed the route of *rebounding.* Crucial to this process is the notion that the people involved have reentered their respective worlds at roughly the same positions as when they left. Throughout this study, a number of factors have been explored that forced some older people to withdraw from various social worlds. When withdrawal occurs, the common-sense notion is that those people probably would never return. Clearly, for several major characters rebounding was a difficult, if not impossible task. Several of them tried and most failed. For example, Erma Martin (Figure 2.4) tried to reenter the ballroom dancing world after she withdrew to escape the amorous desires and marital plans of her dancing partner. She remarked that it proved to be "too much trouble" and "that it just wasn't the same" after a period of inactivity. Similarly, Lucy Anderson (Figure 2.2) sought to return to the same world after a very different kind of problem. The physical injuries she received when struck by an automobile plagued her for months and years. Even though her injury remained chronic, she believed for a time that ballroom dancing was once again possible. She discovered that the demands of dancing simply were greater than her capacity to transcend her injuries. Erma and Lucy each faced quite different problems in their attempts to rebound, but failure for both was the end result.

The experiences of Jack and Gwen Hurling (Figure 3.2) best represent this route. It has been noted that square dancing was a primary activity for them during young adulthood. After many years of inactivity they tried to reenter that world after Jack had sufficiently recovered from his heart condition. In this context it is important to note that successful completion of this route had not been achieved at the time of the interview. They had danced a few times and were convinced that deep integration was possible, but it had not been achieved.

Bailing Out. Finally, it is necessary to focus on a route by which older people suddenly withdrew from certain social worlds. *Bailing out,* then, refers to the fairly radical and sudden shift from intense involvement and deep integration to complete inactivity in that concern. Traveling this route may be the result of economic, social, and interpersonal factors (Allan, 1975; Matthews, 1979; Shanas, 1962). The failures of Lucy Anderson and Erma Martin at rebounding ultimately must be viewed as examples of bailing out. For Erma, following this route was a logical and rational move. However, most of her friends and family simply did not seem to understand her willingness to drop out of ballroom dancing simply because her partner wanted to marry her. Lucy Anderson was familiar with Erma's situation and, perhaps more than any other friend, seemed to understand why such a radical move was necessary to avoid an interpersonal confrontation between Erma and her partner. However, as the following comment illustrates, Lucy continued to view bailing out as an extreme measure.

> You know, I don't really think she had to do that. They are both old enough to tell each other what is going on. From what she has told me, it was the only way she could keep from putting herself in a kind of uncomfortable situation. . . .

Erma's situation is interesting. She believed that withdrawal out of ballroom dancing was perfectly logical, yet her friends and family saw it as tragic. Regardless of personal and social definitions, her situation remained the same. Essentially, she found herself without meaningful social involvement at a time when she wanted to be more active and involved. Eventually, she became involved in a number of other social worlds and other forms of social organization. For a variety of expressed reasons, Erma followed the route of bailing out in most of them.

Evaluating Unconventional Changes

In varying degrees, the older people who followed one or more of the routes of unconventional change did so on the basis of logic and rationales which made sense to them. To friends, family, and others, the changes in social integration occasionally were viewed as tragic or unfortunate circumstances.[3] In an objective sense, this might have been true when the older people involved had followed the routes of backtracking and bailing out. Along these routes they found themselves in situations of less than satisfactory social integration. On the other hand, the route of stalemating situated the older people in circumstances where the social integration achieved was personally satisfying, but viewed as inadequate by others. Shortcircuiting and rebounding were two routes by which greater and deeper social integration was achieved. However, one route had the potential to draw the ire of surrounding social world participants, while the other was viewed as an admirable move by most people.

Clearly, not all who failed to follow the route of conventional change felt they were unhappy, isolated, or disengaged, even though many around them believed that to be true. Some older people seemed quite content with their positions in various social worlds. It is important, then, to take the subjective interpretations of the older people involved into account when making an assessment of social integration. However, it is also necessary to guard against the tendency to assume that all changes in social integration that followed unconventional routes were necessarily positive. Many were positive, but some were not. Therefore, a more accurate portrait of social integration might be achieved by merging the subjective interpretations of older people with an objective assessment of their situation. If the subjective interpretations of people are the only basis upon which situations are evaluated, it is likely that everything they do, are, or might be, will be viewed as positive. As with all people, the aged have a remarkable capacity to make sense of their lives. On the other hand, purely objective evaluations of social integration tend to rely upon numbers of social contacts, kinds of support, proximity of family, and the like. This approach tends to produce a bleak and rather sterile portrait of social life in old age. By merging the two, a more accurate and humane understanding will be the result.

NOTES

1. This conventional ordering of the social types is a reflection of our tendency in Western society to engage in what the anthropologist Dorothy Lee (1950) her termed "lineal codifications of reality." In our culture the logic underlying the social order is that tasks and processes have definable courses, beginnings, and ends. For example, science is conducted via ordered systems of induction and deduction that assume the world is ordered in a lineal, logical, and orderly way. As a result, most assumptions about everyday life similarly follow models reflecting this orientation.

2. While this discussion is concerned with conventional changes, it must be noted that not all such changes are alike, nor that all occur at the same rate. Some changes in status, role, and perspective may be tightly structured and rigidly controlled (Becker and Strauss, 1956; Strauss and Glaser, 1971). For example, such changes in formal organizations or voluntary associations may depend upon adherence to strict rules and procedures. Those higher in a hierarchy of authority may be in the positions to determine whether or not individual actors are able to graduate, advance to new positions, become officers, and the like. Changes in social world integration tend not to be affected by formal structures, processes, and rituals to the same degree as those in other forms of social organization. In social worlds, it is the informal that matters most.

3. The importance of context and situation in self-concept is essential to Ralph Turner's (1976) notion of the "real self" and Louis Zurcher's (1977) "mutable self." In both examples the personal identities of social actors, and the ways they view themselves, greatly depends upon recent events, personal crises, historical period, present company, and so on. Most important in this context is the notion that the self-concept is viewed as something which constantly is changing. Similarly, it is something that may change in ways not understandable to those surrounding the person, as well as following routes that seem illogical to others.

7

INVISIBLE LIVES OF THE AGED

The invisible lives of the aged have been the focus of this study. Essentially hidden from public view because of older people's extensive use of the communications media for maintaining meaningful connections with others, it was argued that involvement in social worlds constitutes an important part of older people's lives. In other words, the shared perspectives and interests that bind people together into various social worlds represent some of the nooks and crannies of modern social life previously ignored in most studies of social integration. Most studies, it was noted, have focused on conventional forms of social organization, wherein people are linked on the basis of formal membership, bureaucratic roles, territorial location, or ascribed traits of some sort. Therefore, the social lives of the aged traditionally have been explored by studying integration into formal organizations, voluntary associations, territorial communities, interest groups, informal groups, families, and so on. With this in mind, this final chapter is devoted to a brief summary of the approach and substance of the study. It will then conclude with a discussion of some practical and theoretical implications of social worlds and the invisible lives of the aged.

SUMMARY

This study of invisible lives began with a brief critique of social integration studies in the sociology of aging and social gerontology. Several strategies were introduced by which the notion of social integration might be rendered problematic. That is, social integration and its presence or absence in the everyday lives of the aged is not easily determined, understood, or evaluated. Then, since the emphasis was on older people's integration into various social worlds, it was necessary to outline a perspective and approach toward social worlds attuned to the nature of the social organizational form. As a start, a definition of the term social world was presented that restricted and narrowed its meaning when compared with the many different usages found in social science and everyday life. For the purposes of this study, a social world was defined as *an extremely large, highly permeable, amorphous, and spatially transcendent form of social organization wherein actors are linked cognitively through shared perspectives arising out of common channels of communication.*

The empirical analysis began by focusing on social worlds in aging lives. It was noted that increased awareness of death among older people has an effect on the personal meanings derived from various social worlds. If specific social worlds are to remain meaningful across the life span, it was noted that the aged must wage a battle to keep up the intense interest, physical stamina, and mental abilities often required of full-fledged participants. To make matters even more problematic, older people may have to do these things in the face of their age peers dropping by the wayside through disability, illness, lack of interest, or death. The battle for social integration into social worlds, then, must be waged on both personal and social fronts.

The focus of the study then shifted to the lives of older individuals in specific social worlds. It was noted that all social worlds probably include participants of many ages, but that some are best characterized by the predominance of one age group over others. The experiences of selected older people were analyzed within youthful, age-mixed, and older social worlds. Whether or not some older people will adopt positions of leadership and importance very much depends upon the numbers and proportions of aged involved. Only rare older individuals manage to achieve such positions in worlds dominated by the young. However, it was argued that in some ways the influence of increasing age on involvement in social worlds is more subtle and less tangible than it is for conventional forms of social organization. Heavy reliance upon media for meaningful linkages, rather than on face-to-face interactions, means that some older people are able to conceal matters of age. By using the mail, telephone, personal letters, and the like it is possible to deal with people who do not know, or perhaps care, about chronological age.

The evaluation of the aged in social worlds continued with the introduction and analysis of eight integrating activities. That is, social integration is achieved and accomplished by engaging in one or more of these activities. The arrangement of the activities implied somewhat greater integration as older people adopted new activities. In other words, the social knowledge that makes up social worlds is organized very much like a whirlpool. Consuming, collecting, creating, performing, marketing, organizing, representing, and evaluating are ways by which this knowledge is learned and applied. The combination of integrating activities found in the lives of the aged says much about their experiences within various social worlds.

Continuing this theme, a set of four social types was introduced that captures the personal experiences of the aged as they become integrated into social worlds of various kinds. The stances of *stranger, tourist, regular,* and *insider* represent important points within the structures of worlds, and each implies fairly distinctive orientations, experiences, relationships, and commitments of those who have adopted the stance. Building upon these stances, the processes by which older people move from one type to the other were outlined. The conventional process was that in which the aged moved through the stances more or less in the order presented. This process conforms to the expectations of many in social science and everyday life concerning how older people should change. In contrast, the unconventional routes of *shortcircuiting, backtracking, stalemating, rebounding,* and *bailing out* were developed to make sense of some changes that were not understood by those surrounding the older people involved, but which seemed perfectly logical and rational to the aged.

Of course, it is important to remember that integration into various social worlds represents only a portion of older people's total connections in modern society. For some older people, involvements in social worlds represent a relatively minor part of their lives. Families, neighborhoods, church groups, and the like may be more important ingredients for their satisfaction and well-being. However, for others, social worlds and their activities are very important and provide great measures of personal meaning. For these people, the identities formed in various social worlds constitute crucial components of their being. However, the relevance of focusing on social worlds for understanding modern social life extends beyond the personal experiences of the aged. In the following section, some implications of this study for understanding other aspects of everyday life will be explored. In addition, some attention will be given to the prospects for social gerontology of better understanding the invisible lives of the aged in social worlds.

IMPLICATIONS

As the preceding summary illustrates, this portrait of the aged and their invisible lives in social worlds is relatively positive and hopeful. It is an image, perhaps, somewhat biased toward social activity and satisfying integration. This was necessary for several reasons. It was theoretically necessary to select older people who were definitely integrated into a broad range of social worlds and other social organizational forms. In this way, the nature of social worlds could be explored. Consequently, the major characters of this study tended to be reasonably satisfied with their personal and social lives in spite of some adversity. It is apparent that many faced severe obstacles due to scarce economic resources, physical disabilities, residential relocation, and changes in family situation. Clearly, the more isolated and socially inactive aged were not a part of the portrait developed. This is obvious, in that the aged living in nursing homes, hospitals, and homes for the aged were excluded intentionally. The experiences of isolation and disengagement among older people were not the focus of this study; the theoretical development of this form of social organization and its relevance for understanding one aspect of older people's lives in modern society was the intent.

However, this theoretical work does have relevance for understanding other aspects of aging and social integration in an ever-changing world. With regard to the more isolated aged, or those dissatisfied with their social lives, the imagery of social worlds holds several possibilities. First, the recognition that communications media may meaningfully link people together is important. If this study accomplishes nothing else, the fact that it grants some legitimacy to the use of media for creating and maintaining interpersonal relations is satisfying. As a result, the guilt felt by some older people because others do not understand the meaning derived from written, visual, or audio sources might partially be alleviated. This is not to say that all uses of mass or personal media bring about optimal social integration, but that it may be better than complete isolation as the alternative. Second, an aura of legitimacy surrounding integration via the media might make the older people involved somewhat less hesitant personally to seek out others with whom they share interests. If the world of soap opera holds the interests of otherwise isolated older people and adds purpose or meaning to their lives, perhaps groups or collectives devoted to such concerns might be encouraged by the powers that be. In this way, face-to-face interaction might be faciliated among what otherwise might be isolated individuals.

More explicit recognition of mass media and its potential for linking older people with others holds additional possibilities. If taken seriously, the spatially transcendent threads that connect the aged with others might be useful means by which information relevant to the everyday lives of the aged might be disseminated.[1] For example, those interested in communicating important information to the elderly regarding personal health, government benefits, personal finance, consumer protection, and social services, might do well to use the linking devices of various social worlds. In this way, the aged who might not attend senior center meetings, read the senior's column in newspapers, or be on specific mailing lists, might be informed. Similarly, the supplemental dissemination of information in these ways might reduce the stigmas associated with traditional locations and sources of such goods or services. In effect, the aged in various social worlds might be more receptive to involvement or participation in various senior programs if they feel they have been sanctioned by their fellow bicyclists, old car collectors, philatelists, or ballroom dancers.

Of course, there is another side to the recognition by social service delivery personnel regarding the involvement of the aged in social worlds. If this kind of integration is better understood, there is the possibility that they might take it seriously in their work. That is, programs and activities for the aged in senior centers and other community programs might encourage integration of their clients into age-heterogeneous social worlds. It was noted earlier that the organizers of senior centers and similar places tend to provide their older clients with bits and pieces of various social worlds. Activities from the worlds of art, music, photography, quilting, and the like might be encouraged. However, for the most part, the older people involved have not viewed these as reflective of legitimate and ongoing concerns by which they might be linked with others. If the organizers of such activities were more aware of the potential for integration into social worlds, perhaps steps could be taken to encourage movement toward relevant social worlds. Talents and skills begun in one context are potential avenues for linkages that may be maintained by the aged outside the context of the senior center or community program where they were first learned. For example, knowing about art or engaging in its production may provide an avenue for meeting new friends should older people have to relocate or perhaps find themselves alone due to the disabilities or deaths of significant others.

Recognition of the social world as a distinct form of social organization has other implications for social gerontology and the study of aging lives. There is need for in-depth analysis of specific social worlds and the place of the aged within them. In certain age-heterogeneous worlds, for example, processes of recruitment (or acts of exclusion) directed toward the aged might be explored. Similarly, the ways by which actions of the aged are accepted, rejected, or legitimized by others needs greater attention and analysis. In line with the logic behind this study, older people should be found in just about every conceivable social world. However, vast differences certainly exist regarding their visibility and involvement. Empirically based comparisons of two or more social worlds would be the next logical step.

Macro-level studies of issues related to aging lives and social gerontology might also make use of the nature and imagery of social worlds. The creation and production of a social object of some sort is the basis of all social worlds. That is, bicycling is the social object around which all the activities, events, processes, and organizations within that world unite. With a small leap upward toward larger-scale analysis, the production of other social objects affecting the aged might be explored. One example would be those social worlds that have come together to produce senior services, mental health, or even a senior center in a specific locale. It is likely that a large number of diverse interests and organizations representing the worlds of business, social welfare, and government have had to come together to produce those social objects.[2] A good deal of negotiation and coordination occurred among representatives defending the unique perspectives and interests of their worlds. Emphasis on the fluidity and emergence inherent in these social processes would reveal much about how these objects were produced. It would also elucidate the ways shared perspectives among competing organizations are accomplished. The imagery of this kind of analysis is present in the study by Carroll Estes (1979) of "the aging enterprise." Her research emphasizes the competition among interests and governmental legislation that has helped create our current social definitions of old age. The ways older people and their lives are viewed by most others truly are social productions based not so much on objective facts as the circumstances into which the old have been placed. These circumstances have been produced by competition and negotiation among various social worlds.

Finally, this study of the aged in social worlds hints at modifications and redirections for future studies of social integration. By focusing on a previously neglected corner of modern social life, it is hoped that future studies might adopt broader, more comprehensive notions of what social integration is, and what it is not. Greater recognition of social worlds in the lives of the aged simply is a small step in this direction. It was noted that other forms of social organization and means of social integration surely lay hidden in the amalgam of behaviors and interactions that make up life in modern urban society (see Lofland, 1975). Increased awareness of these potential sources of integration clearly would lead to more comprehensive studies of the presence or absence of social integration among older people. These are the promises and prospects found in the invisible lives of the aged.

NOTES

1. I would like to acknowledge and thank Warren Peterson for bringing this implication of the study to my attention. During conversation at an Inter-University Training Seminar through the Midwest Council for Social Research on Aging, he mentioned the possibilities of disseminating many kinds of useful information to older people via the linking devices of various social worlds.

2. In other contexts this approach has been applied to and elucidated social and political negotiations that otherwise might have remained hidden. Anselm Strauss (1978) has argued that arenas where many social worlds intersect and negotiate over shared interests represent a fruitful area of inquiry. Carolyn Wiener (1981), in a study influenced by Strauss, studied the politics of alcoholism through this approach. She effectively documented the interorganizational interaction that eventually defined alcoholism as a social problem.

References

ADAMS, BERT N. (1968) Kinship in an Urban Setting. Chicago: Markham.

ALDRIDGE, C. KNIGHT (1959) "Informal social relationships in a retirement community." Marriage and Family Living 21: 70-72.

ALLAN, VIRGINIA R. (1975) "Economic and legal status of the older woman," pp. 23-30 in No Longer Young: The Older Woman in America. Proceedings of the Twenty-Sixth Annual Conference on Aging. Ann Arbor, Institute of Gerontology, University of Michigan: Wayne State University.

ARNOLD, DAVID [Ed.] (1970) The Sociology of Subcultures. New York: Glendessary Press.

ATCHLEY, ROBERT C. (1976) The Sociology of Retirement. Cambridge, MA: Schenkman.

——— (1980) The Social Forces in Later Life. Belmont, CA: Wadsworth.

BABCHUK, NICHOLAS (1978) "Aging and primary relations." Int. J. of Aging and Human Development 9: 137-151.

——— and ALAN BOOTH (1969) "Voluntary association membership: a longitudinal analysis." Amer. Soc. Rev. 39: 767-776.

BARNES, J. A. (1969) "Networks and political process," pp. 51-76 in J. C. Mitchell (ed.) Social Networks in Urban Situations. Manchester: Manchester Univ. Press.

BATES, ALAN and NICHOLAS BABCHUK (1961) "The primary group: a reappraisal." Soc. Q. 2: 181-191.

BECKER, HOWARD S. (1960) "Notes on the concept of commitment." Amer. J. of Sociology 66: 32-40.

——— (1976) "Art worlds and social types." Amer. Behavioral Scientist 19: 703-719.

——— (1982) Art Worlds. Berkeley and Los Angeles: Univ. of California Press.

BECKER, HOWARD S. and ANSELM STRAUSS (1956) "Careers, personality, and adult socialization." Amer. J. of Sociology 62: 253-263.

BECKER, HOWARD S., BLANCHE GEER, EVERETT C. HUGHES, and ANSELM STRAUSS (1961) Boys in White: Student Culture in Medical School. Chicago: Univ. of Chicago Press.

BENGTSON, VERN L. and JOSEPH KUYPERS (1971) "Generational differences and the developmental stake." Int. J. of Aging and Human Development 2: 249-269.

BENGTSON, VERN L., JOSE B. CUELLAR, and PAULINE K. RAGAN (1977) "Stratum contrasts and similarities in attitudes toward death." J. of Gerontology 32: 76-88.

BENNETT, RUTH (1973) "Living conditions and everyday needs of the elderly with particular reference to social isolation." Int. J. of Aging and Human Development 4: 179-198.

————— (1980) Aging, Isolation and Resocialization. New York: Van Nostrand Reinhold.

BERGER, PETER L. and THOMAS LUCKMANN (1966) The Social Construction of Reality. Garden City, NY: Doubleday.

BERK, RICHARD A. (1974) Collective Behavior. Dubuque, IA: William C. Brown.

BERNARD, H. RUSSELL and PETER D. KILLWORTH (1976) "Information accuracy in social network data I." Human Organization 35: 269-286.

————— (1977) "Information accuracy in social network data II." Human Communication Research 4: 3-18.

BILD, BERNICE and ROBERT J. HAVIGHURST (1976) "Senior citizens in great American cities: the case of Chicago." The Gerontologist 16: (1/2).

BINSTOCK, ROBERT H. (1972) "Interest-group liberalism and the politics of aging." The Gerontologist 12: 265-280.

————— (1974) "Aging and the future of American politics." Annals of the Amer. Academy of Pol. and Social Sci. 415: 199-212.

BLAU, PETER (1974) On the Nature of Organizations. New York: John Wiley.

BLAU, ZENA S. (1961) "Structural constraints on friendship in old age." Amer. Soc. Rev. 26: 524-439.

————— (1973) Old Age In a Changing Society. New York: Watts.

BOORSTIN, DANIEL (1961) The Image. New York: Harper & Row.

BRODY, STANLEY J. (1973) "Comprehensive health care for the elderly: an analysis." The Gerontologist 13: 412-418.

BUCHER, RUE and ANSELM STRAUSS (1961) "Professions in process." Amer. J. of Sociology 66: 325-334.

BULTENA, GORDON L. and VIVIAN WOOD (1969) "The American retirement community: bane or blessing?" J. of Gerontology 24: 209-217.

BUTLER, ROBERT N. (1963) "The life review: an interpretation of reminiscence among the aged." Psychiatry 26: 65-76.

————— (1969) "Age-ism: another form of bigotry." The Gerontologist 9: 243-246.

————— (1970) "Looking forward to what? The life review, legacy, and excessive identity versus change." Amer. Behavioral Scientist 14: 121-128.

————— (1975) Why Survive? Being Old in America. New York: Harper & Row.

————— (1980) "The life review: an unrecognized bonanza." Int. J. of Aging and Human Development 12: 35-38.

BUTLER, ROBERT N. and MYRNA I. LEWIS (1973) Aging and Mental Health. St. Louis, MO: Mosby.

CAMPBELL, RITA R. (1977) Social Security: Promise and Reality. Stanford, CA: Hoover Institution Press.

CANTOR, MAJORIE H. (1975) "Life space and the social support system of the inner city elderly of New York." The Gerontologist 15: 23-27.

CAPLAN, G. (1974) Support Systems and Community Mental Health. New York: Behavioral Publications.

CARP, FRANCIS M. (1976) "A senior center in public housing for the elderly." The Gerontologist 16: 243-249.

CAVAN, SHERRI (1966) Liquor License. Chicago: Aldine.

CHARMAZ, KATHY (1980) The Social Reality of Death. Reading, MA: Addison-Wesley.

CHRIST, EDWIN A. (1965) "The 'retired' stamp collector: economic and other functions of a systematized leisure activity," pp. 93-112 in Arnold M. Rose and Warren A. Peterson (eds.) Older People and Their Social World. Philadelphia: F. A. Davis.

CLAUSEN, JOHN and MELVIN KOHN (1954) "The ecological approach in social psychiatry." Amer. J. of Sociology 60: 140-151.

COHEN, ALBERT K. (1955) Delinquent Boys. New York: Free Press.

CRANE, DIANA (1972) Invisible Colleges. Chicago: Univ. of Chicago Press.

CRESSEY, PAUL (1932) The Taxi-Dance Hall. Chicago: Univ. of Chicago Press.

CUMMING, ELAINE (1964) "New thoughts on the theory of disengagement," pp. 3-18 in Robert Kastenbaum (ed.) New Thoughts on Old Age. New York: Springer.

CUMMING, ELAINE and WILLIAM HENRY (1961) Growing Old: The Process of Disengagement. New York: Basic Books.

DAMON, WILLIAM (1977) The Social World of the Child. San Francisco: Jossey-Bass.

DANNEFER, DALE (1980) "Rationality and passion in private experience: modern consciousness and the social world of old-car collectors." Social Problems 27: 392-412.

DAVIS, FRED (1963) Passage Through Crisis. Indianapolis: Bobbs-Merrill.

——— (1979) Yearning for Yesterday: A Sociology of Nostalgia. New York: Free Press.

DENZIN, NORMAN K. (1977) "Notes on the criminogenic hypothesis: a case study of the American liquor industry." Amer. Soc. Rev. 42: 905-20.

——— (1978) "Crime and the American liquor industry," pp. 87-118 in Norman K. Denzin (ed.) Studies in Symbolic Interaction, Vol. I. Greenwich, CT: JAI Press.

DONO, JOHN, CECILIA FALBE, BARBARA KAIL, EUGENE LITWAK, ROGER SHERMAN, and DAVID SIEGAL (1979) "Primary groups in old age." Research on Aging 1: 403-433.

DOWD, JAMES J. (1975) "Aging as exchange: a preface to theory." The Gerontologist 30: 584-594.

ERICKSON, ERIK (1950) Childhood and Society. New York: Norton.

ESTES, CARROLL L. (1979) The Aging Enterprise. San Francisco: Jossey-Bass.

FAGERHAUGH, SHIZUKO and ANSELM STRAUSS (1977) The Politics of Pain Management. Reading, MA: Addison-Wesley.

FINE, GARY ALAN and SHERRYL KLEINMAN (1979) "Rethinking subculture: an interactionist analysis." Amer. J. of Sociology 85: 1-20.

FISCHER, CLAUDE (1976) The Urban Experience. New York: Harcourt Brace Jovanovich.

——— (1982) To Dwell Among Friends. Chicago: Univ. of Chicago Press.

FRANCHER, J. SCOTT (1973) " 'It's the Pepsi generation . . .': accelerated aging and the TV commercial." Int. J. of Aging and Human Development 4: 245-255.

FREEMAN, JO (1975) The Politics of Women's Liberation. New York: Longman.

FRIEDMANN, EUGENE A. and HAROLD L. ORBACH (1974) "Adjustment to retirement," pp. 609-645 in Silvano Arieti (ed.) American Handbook of Psychiatry. New York: Basic Books.

GANS, HERBERT (1962) The Urban Villagers. New York: Free Press.

GERLACH, LUTHER P. and VIRGINIA H. HINE (1970) People, Power, Change: Movements of Social Transformation. Indianapolis: Bobbs-Merrill.

GLASER, BARNEY and ANSELM STRAUSS (1967) The Discovery of Grounded Theory. Chicago: Aldine.

GLICK, IRA O., ROBERT S. WEISS, and C. MURRAY PARKES (1974) The First Year of Bereavement. New York: John Wiley.

GOFFMAN, ERVING (1963) Stigma: Notes on The Management of Spoiled Identity. Englewood Cliffs, NJ: Prentice-Hall.

GOODE, WILLIAM (1957) "Community within a community: the professions." Amer. Soc. Rev. 22: 194-200.

GORDON, CHAD (1975) "Development of evaluated role identities," pp. 61-79 in Alex Inkeles (ed.) Annual Review of Sociology, Vol. 2. Palo Alto, CA: Annual Reviews.

GORDON, CHAD, CHARLES M. GAITZ, and JUDITH SCOTT (1976) "Leisure and lives: personal expressivity across the life span," pp. 310-341 in Robert H. Binstock and Ethel Shanas (eds.) Handbook of Aging and the Social Sciences. New York: Van Nostrand Reinhold.

GORDON, MILTON M. (1947) "The concept of sub-culture and its application." Social Forces 26: 40-42.

GRANOVETTER, MARK S. (1974) Getting a Job: A Study of Contacts and Careers. Cambridge, MA: Harvard Univ. Press.

——— (1975) "Network sampling: some first steps." Amer. J. of Sociology 81: 1287-1303.

GRIFFITHS, ERNEST S. (1939) The Impasse of Democracy. New York: Harrison-Hilton.

GUBRIUM, JABER F. (1975) Living and Dying at Murray Manor. New York: St. Martin's.

HAAS, J. EUGENE and THOMAS E. DRABEK (1973) Complex Organizations: A Sociological Perspective. New York: Macmillan.

HALL, OSWALD (1948) "The stages in a medical career." Amer. J. of Sociology 53: 332-340.

HALL, RICHARD (1977) Organizations: Structure and Process. Englewood Cliffs, NJ: Prentice-Hall.

HANSSEN, ANNE M., NICHOLAS J. MEIMA, LINDA M. BUCKSPAN, BARBARA E. HENDERSON, THEA L. HELBIG, and STEVEN H. ZARIT (1978) "Correlates of senior center participation." The Gerontologist 17: 464-467.

HAUSKNECHT, MURRAY (1962) The Joiners: A Sociological Description of Voluntary Association Membership in the United States. New York: Bedminster Press.

HAVIGHURST, ROBERT J. and RICHARD GLASSER (1972) "An exploratory study of reminiscence." J. of Gerontology 27: 245-253.

HAVIGHURST, ROBERT J., BERNICE L. NEUGARTEN, and SHELDON TOBIN (1968) "Disengagement and patterns of aging," pp. 161-172 in Bernice L. Neugarten (ed.) Middle Age and Aging. Chicago: Univ. of Chicago Press.

HEARN, HERSCHEL L. (1972) "Aging and the artistic career." The Gerontologist 4: 357-362.

HEISS, JEROLD (1981) The Social Psychology of Interaction. Englewood Cliffs, NJ: Prentice-Hall.

HESS, BETH (1974) "Stereotypes of the aged." J. of Communication 24: 76-85.

——— (1979) "Sex roles, friendship, and the life course." Research on Aging 1: 495-515.

HESS, BETH and JOAN WARING (1978) "Parent and child in later life: rethinking the relationship," pp. 241-273 in Richard M. Lerner and Graham B. Spanier (eds.) Child Influences on Marital and Family Interaction: A Life Span Perspective. New York: Academic Press.

HOCHSCHILD, ARLIE RUSSELL (1973) "Communal life-styles for the old." Society 10: 50-57.

——— (1975) "Disengagement theory: a critique and proposal." Amer. Soc. Rev. 40: 553-569.

——— (1978) The Unexpected Community: Portrait of An Old Age Subculture. Berkeley and Los Angeles: Univ. of California Press.

HOLLINGSHEAD, AUGUST B. (1939) "Behavior systems as a field of research." Amer. Soc. Rev. 4: 816-822.

HOYT, GEORGE C. (1954) "The life of the retired in a trailer park." Amer. J. of Sociology 59: 361-370.

HUNT, MORTON (1966) The World of the Formerly Married. New York: McGraw-Hill.

HUSSERL, EDMUND (1950) Ideen zu einer reinen Phanomenologie and Phanomenologischen Philosophie, Vol. 1. The Hague: Nijhoff.

IRWIN, JOHN (1970a) "Notes on the present status of the concept subculture," pp. 164-170 in David Arnold (ed.) The Sociology of Subcultures. New York: Glendessary Press.

——— (1970b) The Felon. Englewood Cliffs, NJ: Prentice-Hall.

——— (1977) Scenes. Beverly Hills, CA: Sage.

JACOBS, JERRY (1974) Fun City. New York: Hold, Rinehart & Winston.

JACOBS, RUTH HARRIET and BETH B. HESS (1978) "Panther power: symbol and substance." Long-Term Care and Health Services Administration Q. (Fall).

JOHNSON, SHEILA K. (1971) Idle Haven: Community Building Among the Working Class Retired. Berkeley and Los Angeles: Univ. of California Press.

KADUSHIN, CHARLES (1966) "The friends and supporters of psychotherapy." Amer. Soc. Rev. 31: 786-802.

—————— (1968) "Power, influence, and social circles." Amer. Soc. Rev. 33: 685-699.

—————— (1976) "Networks and circles in the production of culture." Amer. Behavioral Scientist 19: 769-784.

KANTER, ROSABETH MOSS (1972) Commitment and Community. Cambridge, MA: Harvard Univ. Press.

KARP, DAVID, GREGORY STONE and WILLIAM YOELS (1977) Being Urban. Lexington, MA: D. C. Heath.

KEITH, JENNIE (1982) Old People as People: Social and Cultural Influences on Aging and Old Age. Boston and Toronto: Little, Brown.

KLAPP, ORRIN (1962) Heroes, Villains, and Fools. Englewood Cliffs, NJ: Prentice-Hall.

KLEEMEIER, ROBERT W. (1954) "Moosehaven: congregate living in a community of the retired." Amer. J. of Sociology 59: 347-351.

KLING, ROB and ELIHU M. GERSON (1977) "The social dynamics of technical innovation in the computing world." Symbolic Interaction 1: 132-146.

—————— (1978) "Patterns of segmentation and intersection in the computing world." Symbolic Interaction 1: 24-43.

KORNHAUSER, WILLIAM (1959) The Politics of Mass Society. New York: Free Press.

LAUMANN, EDWARD O. and FRANZ U. PAPPI (1976) Networks of Collective Action. New York: Academic Press.

LEE, DOROTHY (1950) "Codifications of reality: lineal and nonlineal." Psychosomatic Medicine 12: 21-35.

LIEBERMAN, MORTON A. and J. M. FALK (1971) "The remembered past as a source of data for research on the life cycle." Human Development 14: 132-141.

LIEBOW, ELLIOT (1967) Tally's Corner. Boston: Little, Brown.

LITWAK, EUGENE and IVAN SZELENYI (1969) "Primary group structures and their functions: kin, neighbors, and friends." Amer. Soc. Rev. 34: 465-481.

LOCKWOOD, DAVID, (1964) "Social integration and system integration," pp. 121-135 in George Zollchan and Walter Hirsch (eds.) Explorations in Social Change. Boston: Houghton Mifflin.

LOFLAND, JOHN (1971) Analyzing Social Settings. Belmont, CA: Wadsworth.

—————— (1976) Doing Social Life. New York: Wiley-Interscience.

—————— (1977) Doomsday Cult. New York: Irvington.

LOFLAND, JOHN and RODNEY STARK (1965) "Becoming a world saver: a theory of conversion to a deviant perspective." Amer. Soc. Rev. 30: 862-875.

LOFLAND, LYN (1973) A World of Strangers. New York: Basic Books.

—————— (1975) "The 'thereness' of women: a selective review of urban sociology," pp. 144-170 in Marcia Millman and Rosabeth Kanter (eds.) Another Voice: Feminist Perspectives on Social Life and Social Science. New York: Doubleday.

—————— (1978) The Craft of Dying. Beverly Hills, CA: Sage.

LONG, NORTON E. (1958) "The local community as an ecology of games." Amer. J. of Sociology 63: 251-261.

LOPATA, HELENA Z. (1970) "The social involvement of American widows." Amer. Behavioral Scientist 14: 41-48.
——— (1973) Widowhood in an American City. Cambridge, MA: Schenkman.
——— (1979) Women as Widows. New York: Elsevier.
LOWENTHAL, MARJORIE FISKE (1964) "Social isolation and mental illness in old age." Amer. Soc. Rev. 29: 54-70.
LOWENTHAL, MARJORIE and BETSY ROBINSON (1976) "Social networks and isolation," pp. 432-456 in Robert H. Binstock and Ethel Shanas (eds.) Handbook of Aging and The Social Sciences. New York: Van Nostrand Reinhold.
LUCKMANN, BENITA (1970) "The small life-worlds of modern man." Social Research 37: 580-596.
LUNDBERG, GEORGE and M. LAWSING (1949) "The sociography of some community relations," pp. 161-179 in Lawrence Wilson and William Kolb (eds.) Sociological Analysis. New York: Harcourt Brace.
LYMAN, STANFORD and MARVIN SCOTT (1968) "Accounts." Amer. Soc. Rev. 33: 46-62.
MacCANNELL, DEAN (1973) "Staged authenticity: arrangements of social space in tourist settings." Amer. J. of Sociology 79: 589-603.
——— (1976) The Tourist. New York: Schocken.
MAINES, DAVID R. (1977) "Social organization and social structure in symbolic interactionist thought," pp. 235-259 in Alex Inkeles (ed.) Annual Review of Sociology, Vol. 3. Palo Alto, CA: Annual Reviews.
MARSHALL, VICTOR W. (1973) "Game-analyzeable dilemmas in a retirement village: a case study." Int. J. of Aging and Human Development 4: 285-291.
——— (1975) "Socialization for impending death in a retirement village." Amer. J. of Sociology 80: 1124-1144.
——— (1980) Last Chapters: A Sociology of Aging and Dying. Belmont, CA: Brooks/Cole.
MATTHEWS, SARAH H. (1979) The Social World of Old Women. Beverly Hills, CA: Sage.
McCALL, GEORGE and J. L. SIMMONS (1978) Identities and Interactions. New York: Free Press.
McMAHON, W. W. and P. J. RHUDICK (1967) "Reminiscing in the aged: an adaptational response," pp. 292-298 in S. Levin and R. Kahana (eds.) Psychologynamic Studies on Aging: Creativity, Reminiscing, and Dying. New York: International Universities Press.
MEAD, GEORGE HERBERT (1934) Mind, Self, and Society. Chicago: Univ. of Chicago Press.
MERRIAM, SHARAN (1980) "The concept and function of reminiscence: a review of the research." The Gerontologist 20: 604-608.
MITCHELL, J. CLYDE [ed.] (1969) Social Networks in Urban Situations. Manchester: Manchester Univ. Press.

MOTT, PAUL E. (1965) The Organization of Society. Englewood Cliffs, NJ: Prentice-Hall.

MULLINS, NICHOLAS C. (1968) "The distribution of social and cultural properties in informal communication networks among biological scientists." Amer. Soc. Rev. 33: 786-797.

——— (1973) Theories and Theory Groups in Sociology. New York: Harper & Row.

MUNNELL, ALICIA H. (1977) The Future of Social Security. Washington DC: Brookings Institution.

MYERHOFF, BARBARÀ (1978) Number Our Days. New York: Simon & Shuster.

NEUGARTEN, BERNICE L. (1970) "The young and old in modern societies." Amer. Behavioral Scientist 12: 43-57.

PARK, ROBERT E. (1937) "Cultural conflict and the marginal man." Introduction to Everett Stonequist The Marginal Man. New York: Scribners.

PENROSE, L. S. (1952) On The Objective Study of Crowd Behavior. London: H. K. Lewis.

POPLIN, DENNIS (1979) Communities: A Survey of Theories and Methods of Research. New York: Macmillan.

PRATT, HENRY J. (1974) "Old age associations in national politics." Annals of the Amer. Academy of Pol. and Social Sci. 415: 106-119.

——— (1976) The Gray Lobby. Chicago: Univ. of Chicago Press.

PRICE, DEREK J. DE SOLLA (1963) Little Science, Big Science. New York: Columbia Univ. Press.

——— (1965) "Networks of scientific papers." Sci. 149: 510-515.

REYNOLDS, DAVID K. and RICHARD A. KALISH (1974) "Anticipation of futurity as a function of ethnicity and age." J. of Gerontology 29: 224-231.

RIEMER, YOSEF and ROBERT H. BINSTOCK (1978) "Campaigning for 'the senior vote': a case study of Carter's 1976 campaign." The Gerontologist 18: 394-398.

RIESMAN, DAVID, REUEL DENNEY and NATHAN GLAZER (1950) The Lonely Crowd. New Haven, CT: Yale Univ. Press.

RILEY, MATILDA W. and ANNE FONER (1968) Aging and Society, Vol. 1. New York: Russell Sage.

RODSTEIN, M. (1976) "Initial adjustment to a long-term care institution: behavioral aspects." J. of the American Geriatric Society 2: 65-71.

ROGERS, EVERETT (1962) Diffusion of Innovations. New York: Free Press.

ROMAN, PAUL and PHILIP TAIETZ (1967) "Organizational structure and disengagement: the emeritus professor." The Gerontologist 7: 147-152.

ROSE, ARNOLD M. (1962) "The subculture of aging: a topic for sociological research." The Gerontologist 2: 123-127.

——— (1965) "Group consciousness among the aging," pp. 19-36 in Arnold Rose and Warren Peterson (eds.) Older People and Their Social World. Philadelphia: F. A. Davis.

ROSEN, JACQUELINE L. and BERNICE NEUGARTEN (1960) "Ego functions in the middle and later years: a thematic apperception study of normal adults." J. of Gerontology 15: 62.

ROSENBLUM, BARBARA (1978) Photographers at Work. New York: Holmes & Meier.

ROSENFELD, JEFFREY P. (1979) The Legacy of Aging: Inheritance and Disinheritance in Social Perspective. Norwood, NJ: Ablex.

―――― (1980) "Old age, new beneficiaries: kinship, friendship and (dis)inheritance." Sociology and Social Research 64: 86-95.

ROSOW, IRVING (1961) "Retirement housing and social integration." The Gerontologist 1: 85-91.

―――― (1967) Social Integration of the Aged. New York: Free Press.

―――― (1974) Socialization to Old Age. Berkeley and Los Angeles: Univ. of California Press.

ROSSI, ALICE S. (1968) "Transition to Parenthood." J. of Marriage and the Family 30: 26-39.

ROTH, JULIUS (1963) Timetables. Indianapolis: Bobbs-Merrill.

SCHULZ, JAMES (1980) The Economics of Aging. Belmont, CA: Wadsworth.

SCHUTZ, ALFRED (1944) "The stranger: an essay in social psychology." Amer. J. of Sociology 49: 499-507.

―――― (1962) Collected Papers, Vol. 1. The Hague: Nijhoff.

―――― (1970) On Phenomenology and Social Relations. Chicago: Univ. of Chicago Press.

SHANAS, ETHEL (1962) The Health of Older People: A Social Survey. Cambridge, MA: Harvard Univ. Press.

―――― (1970) "Social policy in the field of old age," pp. 149-162 in Tamotsu Shibutani (ed.) Human Nature and Collective Behavior: Papers in Honor of Herbert Blumer. Englewood Cliffs, NJ: Prentice-Hall.

―――― (1980) "Older people and their families: the new pioneers." J. of Marriage and the Family 42: 9-15.

SHANAS, ETHEL and GEORGE MADDOX (1976) "Aging, health, and the organization of health resources," pp. 592-619 in Robert H. Binstock and Ethel Shanas (eds.) Handbook of Aging and the Social Sciences. New York: Van Nostrand Reinhold.

SHANAS, ETHEL, PETER TOWNSEND, DOROTHY WEDDERBUM, HENNING FRIIS, PAUL MILHOJ, and JAN STEHOUWER (1968) Older People in Three Industrial Societies. New York: Atherton Press.

SHIBUTANI, TAMOTSU (1955) "Reference groups as perspectives." Amer. J. of Sociology 60: 562-568.

―――― (1961) Society and Personality. Englewood Cliffs, NJ: Prentice-Hall.

SIMMEL, GEORG (1950) The Sociology of Georg Simmel. Kurt Wolff (ed.) New York: Free Press.

SIMPSON, IDA H. and JOHN C. McKINNEY [eds.] (1966) Social Aspects of Aging. Durham, NC: Duke Univ. Press.

SMITH, JOEL (1966) "The narrowing social world of the aged," pp. 226-242 in Ida H. Simpson and John C. McKinney (eds.) Social Aspects of Aging. Durham, NC: Duke Univ. Press.

STONEQUIST, EVERETT (1937) The Marginal Man. New York: Scribners.

STRAUSS, ANSELM (1961) Images of the American City. New York: Free Press.
—— (1962) "Transformations of identity," pp. 63-85 in Arnold Rose (ed.) Human Behavior and Social Processes. Boston: Houghton Mifflin.
—— (1967) "Strategies for discovering urban theory," pp. 191-203 in Leo F. Schnore and Henry Fagin (eds.) Urban Research and Policy Planning. Beverly Hills, CA: Sage.
—— (1978a) "A social world perspective," pp. 119-128 in Norman K. Denzin (ed.) Studies in Symbolic Interaction, Vol. 1. Greenwich, CT: JAI Press.
—— (1978b) Negotiations: Varieties, Contexts, Processes, and Social Order. San Francisco: Jossey-Bass.
—— (1979a) "Social worlds and their segmentation processes." Department of Social and Behavioral Sciences, University of California, San Francisco. (unpublished)
—— (1979b) "Social worlds and spatial processes: an analytic perspective." Department of Social and Behavioral Sciences, University of California, San Francisco. (unpublished)
—— (1982) "Social worlds and legitimation processes," in Norman K. Denzin (ed.) Studies in Symbolic Interaction, Vol. 4. Greenwich, CT: JAI Press.
—— LEONARD SCHATZMAN, RUE BUCHER, DANUTA EHRLICH, and MELVIN SABSHIN (1964) Psychiatric Ideologies and Institutions. Glencoe, IL: Free Press. (Reprinted 1980, Transaction Books.)
STRAUSS, ANSELM and BARNEY GLASER (1971) Status Passage. Chicago: Aldine.
STREIB, GORDON F. (1974) "Retirement: crisis or continuities," pp. 35-47 in C. Osterbind (ed.) Migration, Mobility, and Aging. Gainesville, FL: Univ. Presses of Florida.
STREIB, GORDON and RUTH B. STREIB (1975) "Communes and the aging." Amer. Behavioral Scientist 19: 176-189.
STRYKER, SHELDON (1968) "Identity salience and role performance: the relevance of symbolic interaction theory for family research." J. of Marriage and the Family 30: 558-564.
SUCZEK, BARBARA (1977) The World of Greek Dancing. Department of Social and Behavioral Sciences, University of California, San Francisco. (unpublished)
SUSSMAN, MARVIN B. (1965) "Relationships of adult children with their parents in the United States," pp. 62-92 in Ethel Shanas and Gordon Streib (eds.) Social Structure and the Family: Generational Relations. Englewood Cliffs, NJ: Prentice-Hall.
SUTHERLAND, EDWIN H. (1937) The Professional Thief. Chicago: Univ. of Chicago Press.
TAIETZ, PHILIP and OLAF LARSON (1956) "Social participation in old age." Rural Sociology 21: 229-238.
THRASHER, FREDERICK (1927) The Gang. Chicago: Univ. of Chicago Press.
TINDALE, JOSEPH A. and VICTOR W. MARSHALL (1980) "A generational-conflict perspective for gerontology," pp. 43-50 in Victor W. Marshall (ed.)

Aging in Canada: Social Perspectives. Don Mills, Ontario; Fitzhenry & Whiteside.

TOLOR, A. and V. MURPHY (1967) "Some psychological correlates of subjective life expectancy." J. of Clinical Psychology 23: 21-24.

TOWNSEND, PETER (1957) Family Life of Old People. London: Routledge & Kegan Paul.

TRELA, JAMES E. (1971) "Some political consequences of senior center and other old age group membership." The Gerontologist 11: 118-123.

—— (1972) "Age structure of voluntary associations and political self-interest among the aged." Soc. Q. 13: 244-252.

TURNER, LOUIS and JOHN ASH (1975) The Golden Hordes: International Tourism and the Pleasure Periphery. London: Constable.

TURNER, RALPH (1976) "The real self: from institution to impulse." Amer. J. of Sociology 81: 989-1016.

TURNER, RALPH and LEWIS KILLIAN (1972) Collective Behavior. Englewood Cliffs, NJ: Prentice-Hall.

TURNSTALL, JEREMY (1966) Old and Alone. London: Routledge & Kegan Paul.

UNRUH, DAVID R. (1979) "Characteristics and types of participation in social worlds." Symbolic Interaction 2: 115-129.

—— (1980a) "The social organization of older people: a social world perspective," pp. 147-170 in Norman K. Denzin (ed.) Studies in Symbolic Interaction, Vol. 3. Greenwich, CT: JAI Press.

—— (1980b) "The nature of social worlds." Pacific Soc. Rev. 23: 271-296.

—— (1983) "Death and personal history: strategies of identity preservation." Social Problems 30, 3.

WARSHAY, LEON H. (1962) "Breadth of Perspective," pp. 148-176 in Arnold Rose (ed.) Human Behavior and Social Processes. Boston: Houghton Mifflin.

WEISS, ROBERT S. (1969) "The fund of sociability." Transaction/Society 6: 36-43.

WHITE, HARRISON, SCOTT A. BOORMAN, and RONALD L. BRIEGER (1976) "Social structure from multiple networks: I blockmodels of roles and positions." Amer. J. of Sociology 81: 730-780.

WHYTE, WILLIAM F. (1955) Streetcorner Society. Chicago: Univ. of Chicago Press.

WIENER, CAROLYN (1981) The Politics of Alcoholism. New Brunswick, NJ: Transaction.

WILDER, CHARLES S. (1971) "Chronic conditions and limitations of activity and mobility: United States, July 1965 to June 1967." Vital and Health Statistics 10, 61.

—— (1973) "Limitations of activity due to chronic conditions United States, 1969 to 1979." Vital and Health Statistics 10, 80.

WILENSKY, HAROLD (1961) "Life cycle, work situations and participation in formal associations," pp. 213-242 in Robert W. Kleemeier (ed.) Aging and Leisure. New York: Oxford Univ. Press.

WOOD, MARGARET MARY (1934) The Stranger: A Study in Social Relationships. New York: Columbia Univ. Press.

WRIGHT, CHARLES and HERBERT HYMAN (1958) "Voluntary association membership of American adults: evidence from national sample surveys." Amer. Soc. Rev. 23: 284-294.

ZURCHER, LOUIS A. (1977) The Mutable Self: A Self-Concept for Social Change. Beverly Hills, CA: Sage.

Index

About the Author

David Unruh currently is an assistant adjunct professor of sociology, and NIMH Postdoctoral Fellow in Mental Health Evaluation Research at the University of California, Los Angeles. He received a B.A. in Education and M.A. in Sociology from Wichita State University. His Ph.D. in Sociology is from the University of California, Davis. He has published essays in the areas of aging, death and dying, childhood socialization, urban sociology, and social interaction.